TALES FROM THE
BEAT

radio

TALES FROM THE
BEAT

COMPILED BY
Joe Lynch and Chris Griffiths

LOCHAR PUBLISHING · MOFFAT · SCOTLAND

© Joe Lynch, 1991

Published by Lochar Publishing Ltd
MOFFAT DG10 9ED

British Library Cataloguing in Publication Data
Lynch, Joe
  Tales from the beat.
  I. Title   II. Griffiths, Chris
  363.2320922

  ISBN 0–948403–23–3

Book design Mark Blackadder

Typeset in 10 on 12 pt Plantin by Chapterhouse, Formby L37 3PX and printed
in Scotland, by Scotprint Ltd., Musselburgh

CONTENTS

ACKNOWLEDGEMENTS

I would like to extend my thanks to all those who took the time to submit material for use in this book. Their names are listed at the rear.

Special thanks are due to:

Sir William Sutherland, QPM, Chief Constable of Lothian and Borders Police for granting permission to carry out the project.

Chief Superintendent Harry Cummings, Lothian and Borders Police for his continued support in the project.

Chris Griffiths and John MacAulay for their encouragement and 'behind the scenes' work.

Norman McLean for compiling the Glossary for the book.

Gillian Rae for the long hours she spent typing out the material for the book.

The children who provided the wonderful drawings reproduced throughout the book.

J LYNCH

The afternamed people have contributed material to this book:

Bob Alston, David Beatson, Alan Bowie, Bernie Boylan, Graham Brown, Billy Burt, Fraser Carroll, Keith Chamberlain, William Davidson, Stevie Gibb, Norman Grant, Chris Griffiths, Colin Harper, Brian Hood, Douglas Jamieson, Alan L Jeffreys, Joe Lynch, Bill Marshall, John MacAulay, William McIntosh, Peter McLaren, Norman McLean, Alan Nicholls, Gerry Neish, Jim Paris, Arthur Pirie, Matt Reid, John Reynolds, Anton Roberts, Jim S. Robertson, John Smith, Kenny Steele, Jimmy Stewart, Davy Sturrock, Davy Taggart, Ian Wark, Dorothy Willimot.

Thanks go out to those who contributed but wished to remain anonymous.

THE ROYAL HOSPITAL FOR SICK CHILDREN, EDINBURGH

The Royal Hospital for Sick Children in Edinburgh (affectionately known as 'The Sick Kids') was opened in 1895 by Princess Beatrice and was described as one of the most perfect hospitals in the United Kingdom.

Today it cares for the demands of 8,500 in-patients and 100,000 out-patients every year. Most of these patients come from the East of Scotland, however for surgery to the newborn, plastic and burns surgery, heart and neurosurgery, children are referred from all over Scotland.

The hospital has a worldwide reputation for the excellence of the service it provides.

A service which is provided not only by the doctors and nurses, but also by the people behind the scenes.

People such as the auxiliaries, who clean the wards, make the beds and cook the meals.

And we must not forget the voluntary workers of 'Radio Lollipop', the hospital's much-loved radio station.

These volunteers not only present the radio shows, but also visit the wards to play games with the children and to read them a bedtime story.

Together they ensure that a child's stay in hospital, which can be a very confusing moment in their life, is as comfortable as possible.

Long may it thrive, long may it survive.

FOREWORD

Over the years, members of the public have always shown a great interest in what goes on in a 'day in the life' of a police officer. Hence the popularity of TV programmes such as '*The Bill*', '*Juliet Bravo*', '*Z-Cars*', and the one which probably started them all off, '*Dixon of Dock Green*'.

TALES FROM THE BEAT will give you an insight into the more humorous, sad and interesting happenings which have been experienced by police officers during the course of their duties.

From their stories you will see that police officers, like most people, commit the occasional 'faux-pas'. They enjoy a laugh and a joke and I am pleased that this is evident in the book as I consider a sense of humour to be an important quality for a police officer to posses.

Police officers must also possess compassion and display a caring touch when the need arises. This too is illustrated in their tales.

Another reason for publishing TALES FROM THE BEAT is to raise funds for charity and all royalties from the book will be applied to the Royal Hospital for Sick Children in Edinburgh.

The hospital, which is probably better known affectionately by all as 'The Sick Kids' and its staff have provided a valuable medical service for children for many years now.

To enable it to provide extra equipment and facilities for the care of its patients, it depends on charitable donations from members of the public. By purchasing this book you have automatically made such a contribution.

I hope you will enjoy reading the tales and anecdotes in this book as well as having the satisfaction of knowing that you have helped 'THE SICK KIDS'.

SIR WILLIAM SUTHERLAND, QPM

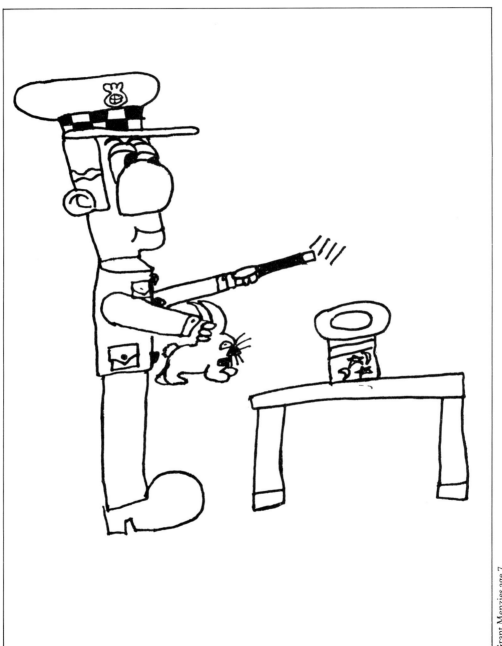

Grant Menzies age 7

ABRACADBRA

One night two police officers found themselves in a sticky situation. They had arrested a man but found they were forced to seek refuge in a doorway as a crowd of men, who were friends of the arrested man, demanded that he be released. When their request was not met the crowd became very hostile and advanced towards the officers, threatening them with physical abuse.

Fearing for his own safety, and the safety of his colleague and the prisoner, one of the officers drew his baton and warned off the crowd. The crowd backed off and began to disperse and then other police officers arrived to render assistance.

Came the day of the court case and one of the officers found himself in the witness box, being questioned by the defence lawyer.

'So, constable, you found yourself backed into a doorway and being threatened by a hostile crowd.'

'That's correct.'

'Tell me what you did, constable.'

'Well, fearing for my safety and the safety of my colleague and the prisoner, I drew my baton and brandished it at the crowd.'

'And what effect did it have, constable?'

'The crowd backed off and eventually they disappeared.'

'So you brandished your baton, a bit like a magic wand and the hostile crowd disappeared,' summed up the lawyer.

'That's just about the sum of it,' smiled the constable.

The next day in the local newspaper the headlines read:

'POLICE CONSTABLE WAVES HIS MAGIC WAND AND A CROWD OF PEOPLE DISAPPEAR'

ANXIOUS MOMENTS

One Saturday morning I was on mobile patrol in a small town west of Edinburgh, with a colleague, when we received a call to return to the station to phone the control room.

We headed back immediately and I phoned through to the control room. I was informed that earlier a young boy had been taken into the Royal Hospital for Sick Children after having accidentally swallowed a number of paracetamol tablets. Whilst at the hospital, he had told the doctor that he had given some of the paracetamol tablets to his two year old sister. Because of her age, unless she received treatment within one hour, the dosage could prove fatal. I learned that the girl was being looked after by her grandparents while her parents were at the hospital.

Without delay we headed up to the grandparents' house. We spoke to the grandfather who told us that the little girl had been taken out in her pushchair by her grandmother.

I explained the situation to the grandfather who suggested several addresses the grandmother may have chosen to visit.

We set out to check them looking out for the woman and child, whose description we had been given by the grandfather.

The two addresses that we had been given were tried but the woman and child had not been there. We returned to the grandparents' house and spoke to the grandfather once more.

He could only suggest one other address. We tried to reassure him before heading off to check it. It wasn't easy, as we too were becoming very concerned for the child's safety.

On checking the address given to us as we learned that the grandmother had been there with the child ten minutes before and had left to go to the local shopping centre.

So down to the shopping centre we sped. We parked the panda and began to stop people, asking if they knew or had seen Mrs Jones and her grandchild. Time was getting on. Half an hour had gone and no one had seen her.

Then our luck changed.

'Yes' one woman told us. 'I saw her round the corner there.'

We ran round the corner and saw a woman walking along with a young child in a pushchair.

'Mrs Jones' we called.

The woman stopped and looked around at us.

'What's wrong?' she immediately asked, probably worried about her other grandchild.

We explained the situation to her. She couldn't believe it because the little girl had showed no signs of illness. We took them to the panda and began to head into Edinburgh.

About two miles into our journey the little girl told her grandmother that she was feeling dizzy. We had twenty minutes left before one hour would have passed.

Knowing that we could not make it through the city traffic in twenty minutes, we contacted the traffic patrol officers who met up with us and took the woman and child into the hospital, blue lights flashing and sirens wailing. Twenty minutes later they arrived at the hospital. The young girl was not very ill and had been sick in the car.

We were relieved to hear later that she had been treated for her condition and was recovering well.

After we had returned to tell the grandfather that we had found them, we headed back to the station for a strong cup of tea.

Sometimes you can't help sharing the anxiety of other people. Especially when the welfare of a child is concerned.

Fiona Steele
Age Six

Fiona Steele age 6

SNIPPETS

During a Scottish Premier Division football match, the ball went flying out of play and hit a police constable on the back, whilst he was patrolling round the pitch.

This delighted the fans immensely and they cheered at the misfortune of the unfortunate officer.

However, after gathering his composure the constable flicked the ball into the air and began to play 'keepie uppie' with it. First of all with his feet, then his knees, then back to his feet. Then he removed his hat, flicked the ball up and headed it back to the football player.

The crowd cheered once more, only this time in admiration for the officer. Little did they know that he was a former professional football player himself.

Grant Menzies age 7

A letter was received at a police station, which had come from a local resident who was complaining bitterly about the speed of cars travelling through the village. The letter was passed on to the inspector in charge of the traffic patrol officers.

He instructed his men to set up speed traps over the following few days.

During that time they caught many speeders amongst whom was the man who had written the letter of complaint in the first place!

The cells of the Sheriff Court were full and the noise coming from them was getting to be a bit much for the sheriff who was sitting in the court above, trying to listen to the witnesses giving evidence. Then he decided that he had suffered enough.

He adjourned the trial and ordered two police officers to go down to the cells and return with anyone who continued to disturb the peace.

The officers returned with one man who had continued to shout and swear at the top of his voice.

The sheriff held the man in contempt of court and sentenced him to thirty days imprisonment.

The next morning, before the court trials began the sheriff paid a visit to the cells.

'Good morning,' he said to the inmates. 'I am the sheriff of this court. Yesterday I sentenced one man to thirty days imprisonment for his excessive noise. Today the tariff will be sixty days.'

That day and every other day that week, the sheriff enjoyed absolute peace and quiet in the court building. Word gets round fast.

A constable attended a call where two neighbours were arguing with each other across the garden fence. As he tried to calm them down one of the neighbours exclaimed, 'He alleged that I swore at him and assaulted him. It's not true. He's always alleging things against me. He's nothing but an "allegator".'

A young probationer, who was married with two young sons, had a habit of saying to them, 'Look boys, a choo-choo train,' if one was passing over the viaduct in the town where he was stationed. The inevitable happened.

One day, while out in the patrol car with his inspector, he spotted a train passing and from sheer habit said, 'Look, a choo-choo train.'

The inspector gave him a peculiar look and replied, 'Yes I know. I've seen one before.'

The sergeant in charge of a small station referred to the Criminal Law Manual as the 'Bible'. He was frequently heard advising younger officers to consult the Bible if they were unsure about a point of law.

Then one day a gentleman called at the station with a question for the sergeant.

'Sorry sir, I can't answer that one offhand, but if you hold on I'll consult the "Bible" '. He got out the Criminal Law Manual and looked up the appropriate page.

'Yes, that seems to be alright according to the "Bible",' said the sergeant.

The man thanked him and before leaving he handed the sergeant a leaflet which read: Salvation Through the Bible.

A youth appeared in court for sentencing. The sheriff gave him thirty days imprisonment and as he was being led out of the courtroom the youth called out, 'I can do that standing on my head.'

The sheriff ordered the youth to be returned to the dock.

'I hold you in contempt of court,' the sheriff told him. 'I sentence you to a further thirty days. Maybe that'll give you time to get back onto your feet.'

The Police Explosives Search Team were searching a large department store prior to the visit of Her Majesty the Queen.

On display at the store was a selection of very valuable vases, especially shipped in for the day.

As one search officer checked through the storeroom he saw a vase which was broken into several pieces. The storeman informed him that it had been broken in transit, but was not as valuable as the rest of the display.

Taking the broken pieces, the officer placed them in front of the display. Then after a word in the storeman's ear he called the inspector over.

'Sorry sir, but I've knocked over and broken this valuable vase.'

The inspector cringed as he asked the storeman how much it was worth.

'£20,000,' was the reply.

A seat was quickly brought in for the inspector, who luckily saw the funny side of it after he had recovered from the initial shock.

Just before the end of the first half of a football match, in which the home team were being beaten 4–0, a police officer saw two youths climbing over the wall of the ground to get in to see the match for free.

'Hey, you two,' he called.

The two youths froze on top of the wall.

'It's no good trying to leave. You'll stay and suffer the second half like the rest of us.'

A robber entered a bank and handed over a note to the teller demanding money. The teller told him that she didn't have any and set off the alarm. On hearing this the bank robber fainted and was arrested when the police arrived.

When the police checked his getaway car, they found that he had locked the keys inside!

Traffic patrol officers attended a road accident on the motorway. One of the first duties they performed was to close off the outside lane with a line of cones. Afterwards, whilst dealing with the accident, one of the officers saw a car approach them and then stop at the line of cones. The car then weaved in and out of the cones until it was stopped by the officer.

When he asked the driver of the car what she was doing she replied, 'I'm sorry, but I thought it was some kind of test that you were conducting.'

One winter's evening, a 999 call was received from a distressed woman.

'There's someone at my front door' she exclaimed. 'They're ringing the doorbell and starting a fire. I'm on my own, can you send someone along quickly please?'

Several officers responded to the radio message sent by the controller and they headed for the woman's house.

To the relief of all, on their arrival they discovered that the caller was the woman's daughter and the 'fire' was in fact the candles she had lit on her mother's surprise birthday cake!

A young constable stood nervously at the passing out parade at the Police College, waiting to be inspected by a senior officer.

When it was his turn to be spoken to, he was asked by the senior officer, 'What height are you, Constable?'

'Five feet, eight inches sir,' was his reply.

'So you just made the height limit?'

'Yes sir.'

'That's good. And what were you before you became a police officer?' asked the senior officer, referring to the constable's previous occupation.

'I was exactly the same height sir,' replied the constable.

Two police officers attended a fire call at a disused building one day. When they arrived they found that the fire service were already in attendance, but to their suprise they were not extinguishing any great blaze.

Instead, they were trying to persuade an old tramp that the old mattress on which he was sitting was smouldering away and he would have to get off it!

The telephone rang and the vetting officer in the police recruiting department answered it.

'Recruiting department, can I help you?'

'Oh, I'm sorry,' replied the caller, 'I was trying to get Edinburgh Airport.'

'This is the police recruiting department,' he was informed.

'Oh well in that case I'm fifty years old but very fit. Do you think I would get a job?'

The manager of the local colliery complained to the police that people were stealing coal from the coal bins in the area and requested passing attention.

One Saturday afternoon two constables came across two young lads coming from one of the bins carrying a sack.

'What's in the sack, son?' asked one of the constables.

'Coal,' replied one of them. 'I got it for my Granny.'

'No' a bad swap son, but what did your Granny have to say about it?' retorted the constable.

A police officer was walking along Princes Street, Edinburgh at the height of the tourist season. His attention was directed towards a very attractive lady making her way towards him. She was an American tourist and she stopped him asking if she could have her photograph taken with him. He obliged and chatted with her for a few minutes.

'Gee,' she said, 'I just love you Scots. I love your friendliness. I love your accent. I love the way you roll your R's.'

The officer couldn't resist it, 'And I quite like the way you walk too,' he replied with a devilish grin.

A major incident exercise was being held and as usual the police had many duties to carry out at it.

Two young constables were given the task of setting up a roadblock, as the exercise involved the movement of terrorists.

Suddenly one of the constables came running down to where one old sergeant was standing and shouted, 'Sarge, sarge, they've captured Jimmy up at the roadblock. I managed to get away.'

'Captured Jimmy eh,' replied the old sergeant, deep in thought. 'That's no' too good. He's got ma piece in his coat pocket.'

A constable decided to go on a foot patrol down the main street of the small town he was stationed in. As he walked along, bidding 'Good morning' to all he met, he was asked by one elderly gent, 'Where's your panda today. Has it broken down?'

'No, I left it at the station. Thought I'd do a foot patrol and let the public see what they're paying for,' replied the constable.

'Well, in that case,' chuckled the old fellow, 'I want my money back.'

An entry on the 24-hour summation sheet made reference to a football match between two struggling Premier Division Football teams.

'NO INCIDENTS, ALTHOUGH SEVERAL COMPLAINTS OF BOREDOM RECEIVED.'

Typing error on summation sheet.

'THE GROUP OF YOUTHS ATTACKED, KICKING THE MAN ABOUT THE HEAD AND NODY.'

(Poor old Noddy. Wonder how Big Ears was?)

An elderly woman hadn't been seen by neighbours for a few days, so they decided to call the police to investigate. An officer arrived at the house and looked through the letter-box. He saw, at the end of the hallway, a frail little woman who was obviously confused at what was happening.

'Open the door, dear,' he called to her. 'I'm a policeman and I'm here to help you.'

The old woman shuffled up to the door and peered at the letter-box.

'I'm no' opening the door,' she said. 'You're too wee to be a polisman.'

A young 'Geordie' Constable was embarrassed when his colleagues found out that his mother was sending him copies of the Beano and Dandy comics. She thought that because they were printed by D C Thomson in Dundee, he would be able to learn the Scottish dialect by reading them.

A police search team were searching a modern art gallery before a visit from a member of the Royal Family. As they checked the building one of the officers accidentally knocked over a piece of modern sculpture which consisted of three wooden pillars of different heights, positioned in a certain manner. As the pillars were not damaged the officer stood them up again in a pattern he thought looked alright.

The Royal visit passed and everyone was happy except for the artist, who was the only one who had realised that the three wooden pillars were in the wrong formation.

A young constable was noting a statement from a man who had witnessed a theft.

'Right, sir,' he said. 'Let me go over this. You saw two men come out from the shop with the stolen goods. They went over to their car, put the goods into the boot and then changed a tyre. After that you saw them go back into the shop, come out a few minutes later with more stolen goods and again put them into the boot of their car. Then they changed a tyre once more.'

The young constable paused. 'Any idea what caused the two punctures?'

'No, no,' said the witness. 'They changed attire. Their clothing.'

Senior officer overheard commenting on a motor cycle officer, 'Yes, you could say he's a middle-of-the-road man.'

A police officer attended at the scene of a road accident. Nothing too serious, just a bump. He parked his panda car in a safe position and put on the lights, hazard warning signals and blue light to warn other drivers of the accident.

As he noted details from the two drivers involved another vehicle collided into the rear of the panda.

The police officer cringed and as he turned to look at the scene, the driver of the offending vehicle jumped out and said to the officer straight away:

'Why did you stop so suddenly?'

Whilst pursuing a man down a busy Edinburgh street, a police officer realised he was not gaining on him and would have to resort to some alternative method in order to effect an arrest.

Knowing that the man he was pursuing was an American, the officer called out, 'Stop or I'll shoot'.

The American must have thought for a second that he was back in the USA. He halted in his tracks and was duly arrested.

One year at the Royal Highland Show, a young police constable found himself on duty near to where some horses were being judged. As he spoke to some members of the public, who were watching the judging, one of the horses broke wind. On hearing the noise it made, one of the women in the crowd became embarrassed and putting her hand to her mouth said 'Oh my goodness.'

Thinking he was doing the honourable thing the young constable turned to the woman and told her, 'Don't worry, dear. Just keep smiling and they'll think it was the horse.'

After a police officer driving a panda police vehicle had skidded, turning the car on its side, then its roof, his colleague in the passenger's seat turned to him and asked, 'Are we still in Kansas, Toto?'

On his arrival at the force, the new Chief Constable decided to visit all the stations in his new force area. On one particular afternoon, he was being shown around a station by its superintendent. On entering the room where the crime patrol officers were based, he found several of them tucking into fish suppers.

'These officers are attached to the Divisional Crime Patrol, sir,' the superintendent informed the Chief Constable.

'And what are you lads doing?' asked the Chief Constable, expecting to be informed of their daily duties.

'Having our piece, sir' said one of them without a thought, as his colleagues prayed for the ground to open up and swallow them all.

Beneath the Sheriff Court in Edinburgh are the cells which hold people who are appearing from custody for trial. From the cells there is a stairway, which leads to the dock of the Sheriff Court. As the prisoners walk up them to their trial, many miss a step intentionally. WHY? Because they are superstitious and the number of stairs there is thirteen.

The young constable was relieved when he was asked to stand down from the witness box after having given evidence for the first time at court. Despite his relief he was still nervous as he left the courtroom at India Buildings in Edinburgh. He tried to conceal the tension he felt as he opened the door at the side of the courtroom and marched smartly onwards and closed the door behind him.

A few moments later the constable re-entered the courtroom from the cupboard and left by the door marked 'EXIT'.

Lisa Anne Cooper

A LUCKY BREAK

Back in the 1960's when the pubs closed at 10pm, about 10.15pm I was walking along my beat when I came across a man slumped over in a hospital wheelchair.

He had his right leg wholly encased in plaster and when I propped him up in the chair, I realised that he was very drunk. Eventually I managed to rouse him and establish how he came to be there.

The man was a patient at a hospital but had fallen and broken his leg in a ward two weeks previously, and was taken to the theatre to have it reset and put in plaster.

On the day in question, he had returned to the hospital for a check-up and afterwards was sitting in his wheelchair in the reception area, awaiting transport. After some time had passed, he had got fed up and wheeled himself out of the hospital and came to a halt outside a pub, where a queue of men were waiting for the doors to open.

He chatted to the men and when the doors opened, one of the men wheeled him into the pub. He had no money but several of the men bought him a drink. Then a couple of them took him on a pub crawl, leaving him asleep in the last pub of the tour.

At 10pm the barman had asked someone to wheel him out, but as no one could get any sense out of him, they had left him in the street where I found him.

Talk about getting a lucky break.

ACCIDENT IN THE SNOW

In the early hours of the morning two constables made their way round their beat, trudging through the thick snow lying on the ground.

They made their way onto the old disused railway line, which was now used as a footpath.

On reaching the part where the footpath went over the old railbridge, they found that it was blocked with several large snowballs.

'Youngsters,' said the older constable, shaking his head in disapproval.

'You're just getting old,' said the younger one. 'Can't you remember doing that sort of thing yourself?'

'Maybe you're right. C'mon let's get them out of the way.'

The two constables began to push the snowballs out of the way to clear the path.

As he was about to push away the last of them the older constable turned to his colleague and said, 'I wonder how big we could make this one? C'mon let's roll it about.'

There they were, two grown men rolling a snowball which was getting larger and larger.

Just then another beat man came walking along the street situated below the old railway line and bridge. Fearing they would be spotted by him the other two constables abandoned their task and hid from view.

Well, the story goes that they unfortunately abandoned the snowball a bit too close to the embankment and down it rolled colliding with the poor beat man on the street below. Purely accidental of course.

Grant Menzies age 7

ADVICE FROM THE SERGEANT

A young probationer and his tutor constable were out on mobile patrol during the early hours of a summer's morning.

As dawn broke they headed over to the local golf course to make a check of the clubhouse and the professionals' golf shop.

After they had checked all around the buildings, which were all secure, they found an old putter and a couple of golf balls lying at the side of the practice putting green.

'We'd better take them back to the station and the dayshift men can hand them in to the clubhouse when it opens' said the tutor constable.

So the probationer constable picked up the putter and the balls, but before going back to the car, he decided to try it out on the putting green.

Just as the young constable was setting himself up for a six foot putt, the sergeant drove up the driveway of the golf club. On seeing the sergeant the young constable missed his putt. By the time he had picked up the balls and headed back to the panda, the sergeant had turned around and was heading off again.

'Did he see me?' asked the young constable.

'Oh, I think he did,' replied his tutor.

'Do you think he'll say anything?'

'I think he'll want to see you when we get in.'

The two officers finished their tour of the town property and headed back into the station. The tutor went straight into the station but the young probationer took his time, dreading having to face his sergeant.

'The sarge wants to see you,' the tutor told him. 'You've to take the putter in with you.'

The young probationer went to the sergeant's office and knocked on the door.

'Come in.'

He opened the door and slowly entered the office.

'You wanted to see me, Sarge?'

'Yes, that's correct. Give me the putter, please.'

He handed it over to the sergeant and stood with head bowed.

'How long have you been in the force now, John?' asked the sergeant.

'Nearly two years, Sarge.'

'Yes, so you've just about finished your probationary period?'

'Yes.'

'Have I always treated you fairly, John?'

'Yes, Sarge.'

'So you'll realise that I have to have this talk with you.'

'I understand, Sarge.'

'Well, John, I'm disappointed with you. Disappointed with what I saw this morning.'

'I'm really sorry, Sarge.'

'Well, listen to my advice. I'll tell you why I'm disappointed with you. That was the worst six foot putt I have ever seen. Now come over here till I show you how to grip the putter properly.'

The young constable didn't know whether to laugh or cry. Meanwhile, his tutor was doubled in two with laughter, having set the whole thing up with the sergeant.

You have to have a good sense of humour in our job.

Grant Menzies age 7

VERY AMAZING GRACE

A 'Geordie' sergeant was sent by his Scottish force on a crime prevention course. The course was to take place in England.

On his arrival at the course one of the first functions was to stand up and introduce yourself to the others. After he had done this, one of the other course members said to him,

'Coming from a Scottish force, I suppose you'll play the bagpipes?'

'As a matter of fact I do,' he announced to the others. 'And I have to practise early in the morning. So don't say I haven't warned you.'

So throughout the first few days of the course the sergeant was called 'Jock' by the others.

Meanwhile, on its way by post was a tape recording of 'Amazing Grace' by the pipes and drums of the Royal Scots Dragoon Guards.

On the Thursday it arrived and later that day Jock told the course, 'I've not practised all week but I'm afraid I'll have to practise early tomorrow morning because I'm playing with the band at the weekend.'

The next morning at 4am, Jock got out of his bed and put the cassette tape into his Ghetto Blaster. Then with the volume turned up, he walked up and down the corridor of the living quarters to the sounds of 'Amazing Grace' and cries of 'Pack it in Jock' from his colleagues.

The next morning at the breakfast table he was confronted with the moans and groans of his course colleagues, who had lost their beauty sleep due to his bagpipe practise.

'Well, I warned you that I had to practise,' said Jock.

'Ah, but what I'm puzzled about,' said one shrewd officer, 'is how you managed to play the pipes and drums at the same time.'

Jock had to put his hands up to the prank.

Grant Menzies age 7

BAKED BEANS SURPRISE

The meal break in the police service is commonly referred to as the 'piece break'.

At a station in Edinburgh, there was one sergeant who day after day, took with him to work, a tin of baked beans with pork sausages.

Each day the men on the shift watched him open up his tin and empty the contents into a pot, heat them up and eat them at his piece break. Day after day the same routine.

Then one of the practical jokers in the force decided to strike. His victim was to be the poor old sergeant.

He arranged, one day, for a telephone call to come through for the sergeant, just as he was about to open his tin of baked beans with pork sausages.

'Telephone call for you in the office, sarge', was the message sounding down the corridor.

Putting his tin aside, he left the canteen and headed off to his office to take the call.

As he did so, the kettle came to the boil and the steam bellowed from it.

'Perfect,' thought the practical joker as he produced a tin of baked beans from a bag (the type without added pork sausages). He then steamed off the labels from both tins and swapped them over, leaving the tin of ordinary baked beans bearing the label from the one which contained added pork sausages.

On returning to the canteen the sergeant continued with his daily routine and opened his tin and emptied the contents into a pot.

'Look at this', he shouted, 'nae bloomin' sausages! I'll be complaining to the manager of the shop I bought them in.'

We never did find out if he made his complaint.

THE PRICE OF TRUE LOVE

It was during the early hours of New Year's Day when my colleague and I attended a call to a house where a Hogmanay party had ended in domestic dispute.

When we arrived we discovered that a fight had occurred between a young man and woman, whereupon she had resorted to inserting a bread knife into her lover's stomach, to claim victory. However, after doing this, both had then realised their love for one another and the man did not wish to make a complaint of assault against his girlfriend. (Talk about Cupid's Arrow or should I say knife!)

Minutes after our arrival an ambulance crew arrived and examined the man's wound. They were of the opinion that it was not serious but would require a surgeon to remove the knife to prevent further damage taking place. As they dressed the wound before removing him to hospital, the woman expressed her desire to go in the ambulance with her boyfriend. The ambulance crew denied her request, fearing that the feud would erupt once more.

I explained to the woman that she would not be able to travel in the ambulance but if she wished I would transport her to the hospital in the police vehicle. She wouldn't listen to me and left the room in tears still stating that she loved him and wanted to go in the ambulance with him.

As the ambulance crew began to remove the man from the house she appeared from the kitchen and through her tears she asked,

'If I was injured would you let me go in the ambulance?'

'Of course I would,' I replied.

'Well,' she said with a determined look on her face, 'you'll have to let me go now,' and proceeded to cut her wrists open with a razor blade which she produced from the pocket of her denim trousers. So she got her wish and was taken to hospital with her boyfriend. Happily both recovered from their injuries.

What price true love?

THE LOOK OF SHEER TERROR

The mortuary is a place which all police officers have to visit during their service. It is never a pleasant experience, in fact many police officers dread having to go to it.

Many years ago, a tragic accident occurred in a small village when a local fisherman was drowned after his small boat capsized. A few days later his body was recovered near the harbour.

The police were informed and the detective officers attended at the mortuary to examine the body, in case any suspicious circumstances surrounded the death.

The body of the fisherman lay on the mortuary table, wrapped in a sheet of black tarpaulin and seaweed.

The younger of the two detectives took out his pocket knife to cut the tarpaulin open. As he did so there was a sudden splashing movement, whereupon the detective dropped the knife and moved swiftly back from the body, his face bearing a look of sheer terror.

'It . . . , it . . . , it's alive,' he gasped.

'Don't be daft lad,' the older detective told him. 'That kind of thing only happens in the horror movies,' and reaching into the tarpaulin he pulled out a flounder, which had got caught up inside it.

THE BISCUIT RUN

I was working my first week of nightshift in a small county town.

About 3am my colleague and I were on mobile patrol when we received a call to attend at the house of an elderly woman, who had reported hearing prowlers.

As we sped along to the house my colleague told me:

'It will probably be a false alarm. The woman is very lonely and she phones in every night about this time to report prowlers. She means no harm, but usually she's heard a cat or even just imagined it.'

When we arrived at the house we saw her looking out of the front window. We checked at the back of the house and her garden and also that of her neighbours. There was no one there and no signs of anyone having been there recently.

My colleague and I then went to speak to her and reassured her that there was no one there. I knocked gently on the door and she answered it.

'Its alright dear. We've checked all about and there's nobody there' I told her. 'Probably just a cat.'

'Oh, there was somebody there.' she nodded.

'Well, he's away now and we'll keep an eye on your house throughout the night' I said hoping that she would feel better.

'You're a new lad aren't you?' she asked.

'Yes, I've just moved out here from the city where I used to work' I told her.

'Come on in then and I'll give you a biscuit' she said turning round and walking through the hallway to her kitchen.

I looked at my colleague and he grinned and then nodded for me to follow her in.

I went in and through to the kitchen. There I was presented with a bag of biscuits and apples.

'Oh, you don't need to give me all these. I'm on a diet' I told her.

'Well, the other policemen can have one with their cup of tea. Go on take them.'

When I joined my colleague in the car he was having a chuckle to himself.

'I didn't want to tell you about that part. I though it would be a nice surprise for you,' he said to me.

The radio sounded, 'What was the result to the call about the prowlers?'

'Six chocolate biscuits and two apples' was the reply.

During my time working in that town I repeated the procedure several times. The call came to be known as the Biscuit Run.

There were never any prowlers on the occasions I attended, but a few reassuring words kept a lonely old lady happy.

BEAT BOXES

The police 'beat boxes' in Edinburgh have been used by beat officers for many years now. (In fact some of them are now listed buildings and cannot be removed). Officers would do their paperwork in them, telephone the station for messages, note complaints from people there, take in found property and even have their piece break in them. The latter could be very unpleasant during the middle of winter, when it was so cold the cheese on your pieces became crunchy rather than chewy.

The beat boxes were also the target of the practical jokers.

One favourite prank always took place just after the festive period. Just about the time when people were sick of the sight of Christmas pud and beat men were tired of having turkey sandwiches for their piece, then the practical joker would search his beat for discarded Christmas fir trees.

When he found the biggest and bushiest one, he would drag it back to the beat box. Not his one though, some other poor beat man's box.

He would then fold the branches of the tree inwards and tie them up with lengths of string. When this was done he would put it in to the beat box and cut the strings, allowing the branches to spring out and return to their natural shape, much to the consternation of the beat man when he returned and tried to gain entry.

On another occasion an officer, who was on car patrol, was called to attend at a particular road where a swan had been injured and was causing chaos to road users.

When he arrived he was able to remove the injured swan from the roadway and decided to put it inside the nearest beat box for safety, whilst he headed off to fetch an SSPCA officer.

Unfortunately he forgot to inform the beat man, who came wandering along and opened the door only to incur the wrath of the angry swan.

And a young probationer almost fainted when he entered the box only to find a man's head sitting in the waste paper bin! If only he had taken a closer look he would have noticed that it was a rubber face mask, stuffed with newspapers with a little raspberry jam to add the finishing touch.

One luxury that was provided in the beat box was a single-bar electric fire. Unfortunately most of them were fitted above head level and therefore most of the heat was lost through the roof. Not much use if you wanted to heat the size tens.

So, many of the beat men fitted a second fire on the floor underneath the small table top which is fitted in it.

Then one of the sergeants took umbrage to these second fires.

'Too luxurious,' he thought to himself. 'It'll encourage them to stay in the box longer, instead of patrolling their beat.'

So with a van, he went round all the boxes and collected the secondary fires and took them back to the station.

Five minutes later he was back round them again trying to figure out which fire came from which beat box. Someone had pointed out to him that the fires he had collected were not police property but belonged to the beat men.

'I think you call it theft,' smirked one officer as the sergeant scurried off before anyone noticed.

Grant Menzies age 7

A LESSON LEARNED AT THE BLACK WALK

As a young probationer constable, I was on duty at Holyrood Palace during the Royal visit week. It was a very hot summer's day and I had been walking up and down the Black Walk, which is an area of the garden wall situated at the rear of the Palace.

I had been there for four hours and I was waiting to be relieved for my meal break. I waited and waited and was rapidly becoming very impatient. As I checked my watch, yet again, I heard a voice say 'No' a bad night, son.'

I looked up and saw an elderly gentleman standing there. He was grey-haired with a ruddy complexion and wore a dark grey suit.

'Have you been here for a while?' he asked.

I must admit, I didn't really feel like speaking to anyone at all. You see a few weeks before I had taken the time to listen to an old man, only to learn that Hitler and his army were going to invade! So you can imagine my apprehension about entertaining this conversation. However,

I did and answered other questions such as, 'How long have you been in the job?' and 'What's on here today?'

Then he told me that he was a retired police officer. He recalled his days in the Edinburgh City Police and then he mentioned that his wife had died six months earlier and that he went for a walk down by the Palace very day, weather permitting.

When we finished our conversation he wished me luck with my career and went on his way, still bearing a broad smile on that weather beaten face of his.

I felt terrible, full of guilt. I had almost let him go on his way without giving up five minutes of my time. All because I was in a bad mood. I really learned a lesson that day. Apart from the fact that it is part of my job to communicate with the public, I realised that someday I might be in the same position and could need someone to talk to.

From that day on I always tried to give some of my time to any old buddies who wanted a natter. Even if it did mean someone telling me that Hitler and his army were going to invade.

CAT IN AN OLD TIN CAN

It was nightshift and I was working in the station when a woman came into the public counter carrying a cat, which had its head stuck inside a tin can.

It looked like a scene from a Tom and Jerry cartoon. She told me that she had found the cat rummaging in a rubbish bin, but was unable to get the cat's head free. My colleague then appeared with a pair of tin snips, which he had in his car, and began to cut open the can, carefully easing the edges outwards to prevent injuring the cat.

Suddenly the cat managed to free itself then before disappearing into the office, bit my colleague and the woman on the hand.

Once inside the office the cat made a bid for freedom and tried to dive out of a window, which was closed.

To prevent any further injury to it, I grabbed my jacket and like a bull fighter, I ushered it to the door. But, before it dashed out of the office, it jumped onto my jacket, climbed up the sleeve and bit me on the hand. The cat then made good its escape from the station.

Meanwhile, arrangements were being to have the three of us taken to hospital to receive anti-tetanus injections. So much for being an animal lover.

CLOSE ENCOUNTER

As a sergeant in the Identification Branch of the CID, one of my duties involved photographing the scene of a crime or an incident such as a fatal accident or suspicious fire.

But I never thought I would see the day when I was called to take photographs of a piece of grassland where a spaceship had allegedly landed.

The incident took place one Friday morning in November, 1979, in a forest clearing in Livingston, West Lothian.

The man who experienced the close encounter was a forester who was making an inspection of the forest at the time.

About 10.15am he was walking along a forest track, accompanied by his dog, when he rounded a corner and found himself confronted with what he described as a spaceship. It was a hemispherical dome with a flange at the equator. It was dark grey in colour with the surface texture changing from rough to smooth and shiny, as though it was trying to camouflage itself.

The man could not tell whether it was hovering or had landed on the ground.

As he stood staring at it two smaller objects appeared from it. They were spherical with several legs radiating from them. They moved towards him and stopped either side of him, attaching a leg to the sides of his trousers. The spheres began to pull him forwards and he then became aware of a strong burning smell. He began to choke and fell to the ground where he lost consciousness.

When he recovered about twenty minutes later, the spacehip had vanished and only his dog, who was barking wildly, was by his side. He tried to speak to his dog but found that he had temporarily lost his voice. When he tried to stand up and walk, he found that his legs would not support him and he had to crawl for about 100 metres until he regained his strength.

He was suffering from a terrible headache which lasted several hours and intense thirst which lasted several days. His trouser legs were torn at the sides.

The encounter was reported to the British UFO Research Association, who worked with the police on the subsequent investigation.

My duty was to photograph the landing area. There were markings in the grass but they were isolated and did not lead anywhere. The ground beneath the grass markings was not broken.

The man who experienced the encounter was a mature, sensible and well respected forester, who had no great interest in UFOs and was not the type to lie or play practical jokes.

Researchers looked at the possibility of the man suffering from an epileptic fit and at the same time experiencing a natural phenomena such as ball lightning or an astronomical occurrence.

Others, like the man concerned, firmly believe that it was a spaceship landing.

If you have any doubts about the incident, remember the markings in the grass. They show that something very real was sitting in that clearing.

The question still remains – 'What?'

C.O'Neill age 13

COAT OF ARMS

A newly promoted superintendent stood proudly within the ground of a Premier Division football club one Saturday afternoon, before the start of the match. He boasted to other senior officers about the quality of his brand new greatcoat, which he had purchased personally.

After the game had finished he was smart and impressive-looking as he took command of a street disturbance which involved opposing football supporters. The scene was hectic.

The roads were jammed with cars and the streets were crammed full of people leaving the football ground. A large number of police officers were called in to deal with the situation and under the excellent direction of the superintendent, they were beginning to gain control.

However, to this day the Superintendent regrets giving out one order to his officers. He learned that you do not keep a whole sleeve on a new coat if you wave an instruction to a police dog handler directly in front of the nose of his dog!

COCO THE CLOWN AND THE PARKING CONE

It was Saturday night and the pubs were emptying. My colleague and I came across the usual crowd of rowdies. You know the type. A few pints too many and they change character. One becomes Frank Sinatra and wants to sing his entire list of hits, another becomes Rambo despite being a foot smaller than everyone else and then there is Coco the Clown.

They were getting a bit rowdy so we told them to keep the noise down and move on. This they did but as soon as they were out of reach they started again.

We made our way towards them and on seeing us they moved on and quietened down. We continued to follow them at a leisurely pace.

Then he appeared from the crowd. Coco the Clown had spotted some parking cones and headed straight for them.

Picking one up, he put the narrow end to his mouth, using it as a loud-hailer.

'This is the police,' he called through it, much to the delight of his friends.

'Keep moving on and keep the noise down' he continued, his comments obviously directed at us.

We had heard it all before and it was like water off a duck's back.

Just then, a man passed by on a bicycle.

'I wouldn't do that if I were you mate,' he called to Coco.

'It's alright pal, the polis are too far away to catch me.'

'I don't mean that,' the man said, 'but that dog over there has just peed on those cones.'

Suddenly Coco didn't feel like clowning around anymore and looked as though he was going to be sick.

Stuart Reid

COURTROOM CAPERS

For a few years I was one of a team of police officers who worked in the Sheriff Court. Our duties were to take prisoners from the cells to the courtroom and if they were sentenced to imprisonment, take them back down to the cells again (hence the saying that the person was 'sent down' by the judge as there are a set of stairs which lead from the courtroom straight down to the cells).

One of the pleasures I experienced was being present in the court when one particular sheriff was on duty. He was a very shrewd man with a tongue and a wit as sharp as a razor blade.

At one trial a man was found guilty of many charges of theft. His lawyer made an appeal to the sheriff.

'M'Lord, my client came through to Edinburgh from his home town near Glasgow in an effort to find work and to send money home to his poor family. He did not succeed in his mission and through desperation he resorted to crime to obtain some money. I would ask you to be lenient with him in your sentence and free him from this court, so that he can return to the west, to be near his family.'

Now the sheriff had heard and seen this all before. He had made his mind up. This man was going to jail.

'Does Barlinnie sound far enough west for you?' the sheriff then asked the lawyer, who instantly got the message.

On another occasion, when the person who should have been on trial did not appear, a lawyer stood up and informed the sheriff that sadly his client could not be at court that day, as he had died two weeks earlier.

'No doubt he will now be tried at a higher court than mine. Next case,' retorted the sheriff as he raised his eyes heavenwards.

Lawyers could be just as quick witted though. I remember one day a case of 'careless driving' and the sheriff that day made use of toy cars to enable the witnesses to demonstrate the movements of the vehicles involved.

'And what happened next?' the witnesses were asked.

'An ambulance arrived and took the injured person away.'

'Oh,' said the sheriff, 'I don't have an ambulance. Mr Sheriff Clerk, go out and buy me a toy ambulance.'

The court was adjourned until a toy ambulance was bought and then the case was concluded.

During this time one particular lawyer was waiting at the back of the court for the next trial to start and had become very frustrated and angry.

The next case was called and up stood the lawyer.

'M'Lord, I represent the man in this case. He is charged with indecent exposure. Would you like to send the sheriff clerk out to buy an Action Man and a "Cindy Doll" so that the witnesses can demonstrate what happened?'

Sam Alcorn age 5

DEEP TREADS

I remember my first day on duty. There I was, my uniform pressed with creases so sharp they could cut. My brand new Dr Marten shoes were highly polished and the soles with their deep treads hardly even worn. Pity it was raining though. Still, it gave me a chance to try out my new raincoat.

It was a beat in the city centre that I was working on and it had taken me all my time to find the beat box to start from. So you can imagine how I felt when I received a radio message to make my way to the station to meet my divisional commander. I didn't know how to get there!

The senior constable I was with gave me directions and I set off on my journey.

As I rehearsed in my mind what I would say to the divisional commander, I failed to pay attention to where I was placing my feet. Suddenly I slipped as though I had stood on a banana skin.

It wasn't a banana skin though. Someone had been out with their alsation. (Actually, I think it must have been an elephant!)

There I was, heading off to see the divisional commander and the treads of my right Dr Marten shoe were filled with brown matter (for want of a better phrase).

Oh, it would have been easily remedied if I had been in an area with grass embankments or fields nearby. But it was the city centre and I was surrounded by office blocks and hotels, and except for the weeds growing through the cracks in the footway, there wasn't a lot of green stuff about.

I couldn't help but notice passers-by looking at me in a strange manner as I walked along dragging my right foot in an effort to scrape the stuff from my shoe.

Eventually I found a pile of leaves which assisted me in my task, finishing it off with a paper handkerchief.

So much for deep treads on my shoes.

DENTAL TREATMENT

Two police officers received a 999 call regarding a man armed with a knife, who was threatening people in the street.

They attended immediately and saw the man standing on the roadway armed with a kitchen knife. When the officers attempted to arrest him a struggle ensued and all three ended up rolling about on the ground.

As they began to overpower him, tragedy struck. One of the officer's dentures went flying out of his mouth and landed on the footway, near to an old woman who had been washing her front doorstep.

When they finally managed to pin the man down and call for back-up, the toothless officer called to the old woman.

'Could you give my teeth back, please.'

'Nae bother son,' she replied.

Then picking them up she gave them a rinse in her bucket of water, before going over to the officer (who was kneeling on the ground holding onto the man) and sticking them in his mouth!

IN THE DOG HOUSE

Prior to the High Court trial of a high security risk prisoner, the court building was searched by a police search team and a dog handler. The dog handler was assisted by his loyal and hard-working springer spaniel, especially trained for finding explosives.

While searching on the level beneath the courtrooms, the excited spaniel worked like a beaver. It scurried from room to room, under and over furniture, in and out of every nook and cranny.

The handler followed his dog, desperately trying to keep up with the hundred mile per hour pace. He watched the searching spaniel sprint towards the door of a toilet and sensed immediately that the dog would not be able to stop in time. The dog's front paws slammed down hard on the linoleum floor but it had braked too late. Out of control, it skidded towards the piece of wood which was propping the door open. Its hind quarters crashed into the door and the prop clattered to the floor.

The handler went into a suicidal dive for the door but he was too late. It was not the slam of the door that perturbed the officer but the click sound that came from the lock.

It was a very embarrassed handler who was forced to ask the security people to let his dog out of the toilet.

WHAT THE EYE CAN'T SEE

A seasoned, old head constable was involved in the arrest of a group of poachers. His actual task was arresting the man who was acting as the look-out.

When the case came to trial, the old constable found himself in the witness box being questioned by the defence lawyer.

'So, Constable, you have already told the court that my client was part of the gang of poachers and that his job was acting as the look-out.'

'Yes, that's correct.'

'Can you explain why you came to this conclusion, Constable?'

'I saw your client hiding behind a wall and he was looking all about and signalling to the others when to move.'

'Well, Constable, it surprises me that my client would be used as a look-out because my client has only one eye. In fact he is only partially sighted in that eye and is a registered blind person. Does that not surprise you, Constable?'

'No sir, it does not surprise me.'

'Come, come, Constable. You say my client was a look-out, yet you are not surprised to hear that he is a registered blind person. Why then, Constable, are you not surprised?'

'Because,' said the constable, 'he didn't see me coming when I arrested him.'

'No more questions,' said the red faced lawyer as the courtroom erupted with laughter.

A FOXY TALE

A young officer based at a small police station in Edinburgh was renowned for his practical jokes. In an effort to get his own back another officer decided to carry out the very sick joke of tying a dead fox to the rear of the joker's car.

At the end of his shift, the keen eyed joker spotted the carcass and promptly walked back into the station saying 'I'll get £15 for that fox at an exclusive Edinburgh fur shop.'

The officer who had tied the fox insisted on its return.

It was later rumoured that a certain officer was invited, in the strongest possible terms, to leave an Edinburgh fur shop along with a strong smelling prize.

A GIFT FOR THE SARGE

The practical joker was not necessarily confined to the rank of constable. Sergeants also often liked to play their tricks on other people, but did not enjoy the tables being turned on them. But that's exactly what happened to one sergeant.

The men on his team were getting a bit fed up with his pranks and decided to get their own back on him. It was just a matter of waiting for the right moment to arrive.

Then the time came for the sergeant to take his annual leave.

'What are you going to do during your leave?', enquired one officer.

'Oh, I'll probably do a bit of DIY around the house and get my garden into shape. I would really like to get a garden statue or a sundial and some new shrubs for it,' replied the sergeant.

The following week the sergeant went on leave and his team began on the nightshift (the best shift to play practical jokes on someone).

Keeping in mind the sergeant's desire to have a statue in his garden, they began to search the streets and rubbish skips for something appropriate. One officer came across an old tailor's dummy. Another found an old toilet bowl. They quickly set to work.

The next morning as the sergeant lay sleeping, he was awakened by the sound of car horns. When he got up and looked out of his bedroom window, he saw why the passing motorists were sounding their horns. Sitting in the middle of his lawn was the toilet bowl and on top of it, in the pose of the Thinker, was the tailor's dummy.

The lads had saved him the bother of buying a statue for the garden. Unfortunately, it wasn't to his liking.

YOU'VE GOT TO HAND IT TO THE SHERIFF

After a sheriff had heard the evidence in a trial, he found a man guilty of a crime of dishonesty.

It was now the turn of the man's lawyer to make a plea for leniency to the sheriff, who was about to pass sentence.

'M'Lord, my client is well aware that what he did was wrong but he would like the court to know that it was done out of desperation and frustration, caused by the fact that my client cannot find employment.'

'And what is the reason for his failure in finding employment?' asked the sheriff.

'M'Lord, my client has a disability in his right hand. He finds great difficulty in picking things up, which prevents him from doing any manual work.'

'Could I see your client's attempts to pick up some articles?' the sheriff asked.

The lawyer agreed and placed his pen on the table whereupon the man made a pitiful attempt to pick it up with his right hand, but failed miserably.

The sheriff asked him to pick up an apple which he produced from his desk drawer, but the result was the same.

The sheriff thought long and hard and then told the lawyer that he would adjourn for lunch and pass sentence afterwards.

During the lunch break the sheriff decided to go for a walk to get some fresh air and give him a clear mind to make his decision with.

The trial resumed after lunch and the sheriff addressed the lawyer.

'I have had time to think about your client's condition and would like to ask him a few questions.'

'Certainly, M'Lord,' replied the lawyer.

'Would your client be able to pick up a newspaper with his right hand?'

'I don't think so, M'Lord.'

'Well, what about a glass of beer?'

'Most certainly not, M'Lord. He really is unable to use it to pick up anything.'

'Is that so?' said the sheriff. 'Well that is very strange. You see, during the lunch break I decided to take a walk in the fresh air to help clear my mind, so that I would be able to make the correct decision about the sentence I should impose upon your client.

As I passed by one of the public houses nearby, I happened to look through the window, whereupon I saw your client sitting inside. And lo and behold he did not seem to have any difficulty in picking up a newspaper or his glass of beer with his right hand. So you see the fresh air did clear my mind.

I sentence him to three months' imprisonment.'

HEADING FOR TROUBLE

The month was January, a few days after the New Year celebrations were over.

I was the sergeant at a station in a county town and was sitting in my office when the bell rang at the public counter.

I went through to attend to the caller only to see two of the town's well-known characters. One of them had his head shaved and it bore several sets of sutures. The fact that he had a small tufted beard made him look very peculiar indeed.

He had come into the station to find out if anyone had handed in a watch which he had lost. As I checked the Found Property list I could not contain my curiosity.

'What happened then?' I asked.

His mate got his say in first.

'He's had his heid put on upside down,' he laughed.

'You shut up. It's your fault anyway,' the bearded one growled.

'How is it his fault?' I asked.

He stared daggers at his mate, who was still laughing away and then began to give me his tale of woe.

'Well, on Hogmanay we went out to have a few drinks before the bells and we ended up having a bit too much. After the bells we decided to go for a walk to sober up and ended up beside a reservoir.'

His mate was now laughing uncontrollably and got a swift kick in the shin from the one telling the story, which stopped him momentarily.

'We decided to go in for a New Year's swim.'

'My goodness, it was absolutely freezing that night,' I interrupted.

'Aye but you don't realise that when you're steamin',' he carried on. 'We stripped off and climbed onto a rock to dive in.'

'So what happened, did you slip on the rock and strike your head on it?' I asked.

'No, I dived into the reservoir only to find out that it was frozen solid with six inches of ice and I burst me heid open.'

His friend returned into fits of laughter.

'So how was it his fault?' I asked.

'Well, we tossed a coin to see who would go in first. He won but gave me the honour.'

HOLY SMOKE

It was a quiet, sunny, summer's afternoon, when the Fire Service and Police Service were called to attend at one of the churches in the area regarding a fire in the bell tower.

The police were first on the scene and when the officers got out of the panda car they could see clouds of black smoke swirling round the bell tower. They called at the church house to alert the vicar.

The vicar informed them that no one had been in the bell tower and if there was anyone there it would probably be an old tramp. The officers pointed out the clouds of smoke coming from the bell tower and the vicar agreed to give them access in case there was someone trapped in the fire.

As they set off up the stairs of the bell tower, the Fire Service arrived. The senior fire officer joined the vicar and the two police officers in their journey to the top of the tower. Then a few seconds later followed two firemen with a hose reel.

As they reached the top they all began to secretly wish that someone had brought the oxygen, so tall was the tower.

The vicar opened the door of the belfry and stood aside to allow the police and fire officers to enter. This they did but to their surprise they found the place all in order. The vicar, on hearing the news, raised his eyes heavenwards and said, 'Thank you Lord,' believing that divine intervention had saved the church from burning to the ground.

However, when they looked out of the windows they were to solve the mystery. A swarm of midges had formed a black cloud by flying in and out and round about the bell tower!

Grant Menzies age 7

A HOLD-UP WITH THE PROCEEDINGS

A police inspector, who was working in plain clothes, decided to go to the bank during his lunch break.

He spoke to the lady cashier and told her that he would like to make a withdrawal, although the bank was not his local branch. She told him to fill out a withdrawal slip and she would contact his local branch to authorise payment.

The inspector took a withdrawal slip from the pile at the counter and filled it out. He handed it over to the woman and then stood to the side to allow other customers to be served.

BEAT

The woman in turn passed the withdrawl slip to the accountant to have the payment authorised.

Whilst the inspector was waiting, a uniformed constable walked into the bank and seeing each other they began to converse.

The inspector then heard his name being called and when he looked over at the service counter he saw the accountant and other members of the staff laughing uncontrollably.

As he walked over to the counter he began to wonder what all the hilarity was about.

'Excuse me for asking,' he said to the accountant, 'but what's all the laughter for?'

'I'm sorry,' said the accountant, gathering himself together, 'but please read what's on the back of your withdrawal slip.'

The inspector did so and to his surprise he saw the words:

I HAVE A GUN. HAND OVER THE MONEY.

'We were just about to call the police when someone recognised you as the police inspector and saw you speaking to another policeman,' the accountant told him.

Obviously some youngster had written the demand on a withdrawal slip and placed it amongst the other slips as a prank.

Grant Menzies age 7

LOOK OUT BELOW

During the visit of Pope John Paul II to Scotland, preparations were being made for his tour of Edinburgh. One of the places that he was due to attend at was the Roman Catholic Cathedral.

About a week before the day of the event a chief superintendent visited the cathedral to familiarise himself with the building and discuss arrangements with the local priests.

The chief superintendent was not a member of the Catholic church and on entering the cathedral he was immediately impressed by its architecture and decor.

He was greeted by one of the priests and they both began to walk down the aisle, the priest leading the way. As they walked, the priest began to explain to the chief superintendent what would take place on the day of the Pope's visit.

Although he was taking in every word that the priest said, the chief superintendent could not stop himself from looking around at the paintings, statues and stained glass windows.

Then suddenly the chief superintendent stumbled over something and landed on his derriere in the middle of the aisle. When he looked round from his seated position he discovered what had caused his fall.

He had stumbled over the priest who had stopped and genuflected in front of the altar.

CONDEMNED MAN'S REQUEST

It was about 2am and I was on mobile patrol with a colleague when we came across a man lying in the road. It had been raining and he was soaking wet, but also drunk out of his mind. He could hardly stand, but from his slurred speech we established that he stayed nearby.

We put him in the panda car and although he had committed the offence of being drunk and incapable of taking care of himself, we decided to see if there was anyone at his home address that could take care of him, rather than put him in a cell for the night.

As we drove off he asked in his drunken gabble, 'Are you locking me up?'

'No, we're taking you home,' he was told.

'No, lock me up,' he requested.

'Don't be silly. We'll take you home to your wife.'

'No, please lock me up. I don't want to bother her.'

We kept on going and when we arrived outside his house he began to plead with us.

'Please, lock me up. Don't disturb my wife. Lock me up.'

He had started to sober up very quickly and appeared terrified to face his wife.

We eventually got him out of the car and helped him down the path to the front door of his house. Once more he begged, 'Please don't wake her up. Lock me up instead.'

We rang the door bell and eventually his wife came to the door.

'Is this your husband?' I asked.

'Yes' she replied, staring daggers at him, whilst he stood like a scolded child, staring down at the ground.

'Thank you officers' she said to us and then turning to her husband she told him, 'You get inside. I'll teach you to embarrass me with your drunken exploits.'

As we left him in her capable hands he turned to us and said, 'I told you to lock me up, but you wouldn't listen.'

Sometimes you just can't please everyone, no matter how kind you try to be.

MAN'S BEST FRIEND

I was on foot patrol when I received a call to attend at the corner of the street where a man would meet me, to report that he had been assaulted.

I went along and out from the telephone box there stepped a small rotund man who had dog with him.

'Iz me, pal' he slurred. 'Me. Am the one who's been assaulted.'

He was obviously drunk, but didn't have visible signs of injury.

'Do you require medical attention?' I asked him.

'No, am alright. Just a dunt on the back of ma heid,' he replied.

I took another step backwards as I was being overcome with the smell of alcohol from his breath.

I started to note details about him. He explained that he had been walking along the road, minding his own business (although I later found out he had been shouting abuse at passers-by), when someone had punched him on the back of the head and ran off. He did not see his attacker.

'Did anyone else witness the attack?' I asked.

'Aye.'

'Who was it then?'

'Rover, my dog.'

'Your dog, sir?' I queried.

'Aye, he's a witness.'

I looked down at his dog who wagged its tail at me as if to agree with what his master had said. I tried to explain that the dog couldn't be a witness, but he insisted to the point of becoming aggressive.

I decided to humour him.

'Right sir, so your dog saw the attacker.'

'Oh, he did and what's more he knows the person.'

'How do you know this?'

'Because, he didnae bite him. You see he disnae bite people he knows, so he must have recognised him.'

I looked down at the dog and once more he wagged his tail in acknowledgement.

'Pity your dog wasn't a pointer or he could have pointed the attacker out,' I said, hoping that he would see the funny side to it. Luckily he did.

'Oh aye,' he laughed. 'I guess you'll just have to get Dr Doolittle to speak to him' and he went away with his best friend and witness.

MEDIUM POWER

I remember the day I received a call to attend at a house which had been broken into.

When I got there I began noting details from the occupier, a lady. To my surprise when I asked her what her occupation was she told me that she was a medium.

I looked at her with doubt written all over my face.

'No, I'm not joking, officer. That's what I really am.'

I noted it down, but I obviously didn't look convinced.

'Let me prove it to you,' she said.

She stared at me for about a minute and then said to me,

'You're married. Your wife's name is Jean. You have two children, a boy named John aged nine, and a girl, Michelle, aged eleven. Do you wish me to go on?'

'No thanks,' I said, 'I believe you.'

Mind you, she might have told me who had broken into her house!

MURKY WATERS

I remember the time that I was sent to attend at a house to see a woman who wished to make a complaint.

I was new to the area but the others on the shift team were not and knew the woman concerned. She had the reputation of having one of the town's dirtiest and untidiest houses. I didn't know this and was nominated to attend the call.

I went along to the block of flats where she stayed. Her house was on the first floor and when I got to the front door I found it ajar. I knocked on it and a voice called, 'Come in.'

On entering the house I realised that I would have to be very careful where I put my feet, and the smell wasn't exactly aromatic to say the least. The place was filthy. To describe it in full would require more than just a few words.

Sitting on a chair in the livingroom, with her feet in a basin of water, which was as black as coal, was the woman.

As I noted the complaint I couldn't help noticing the way she kept wiggling her toes in the water, which was getting dirtier and dirtier.

Then I realised why. As she finished off her statement to me, she picked up a small knife from the floor, put her hand into the basin of water and pulled out a potato and began to peel the skin from it!

If that wasn't bad enough, she then offered me a cup of tea. I politely declined.

A CASE OF MISTAKEN IDENTITY

I remember one day I was working in the Sheriff Court. Nothing was going right. Some of the accused persons had failed to turn up. Some of the witnesses had failed to turn up. The sheriff was not a happy man.

'Are you going to get a trial started today or shall we all just go home?' he scowled.

'Yes, M'lord,' said the procurator fiscal. 'The next case is one of an assault and we are ready to start.'

'Very well,' said the sheriff, 'begin immediately.'

The accused person was placed in the dock and the trial began. The procurator fiscal asked for the first witness to be called and for the sake of my story we'll call him Joe Bloggs.

The court usher called out, 'Witness Joe Bloggs'. There was no response. He then went from the door of the court room into the witness room. 'Is Joe Bloggs here?' The people sitting in the witness room looked blankly at each other and shook their heads from side to side.

The court usher left the witness room panicking as the sheriff began to drum his fingers on the table, his patience beginning to fray. Then the court usher saw a man coming out of the toilet.

'Are you Joe Bloggs?' he asked him.

'Aye, that's right,' said the man.

'Well come on, you're required in the court. Now hurry up, the sheriff's in a bad mood so don't upset him.'

The man tried to ask a question of the court usher, but he would not listen and hurried the man into the court room and up into the witness box.

As a bewildered Joe Bloggs looked all around the room, the sheriff stood up and said, 'Look at me, raise your right hand and repeat after me.'

Joe Bloggs, on seeing the anger in the sheriff and remembering the court usher's advice, did as he was told and took the oath.

The sheriff sat down and the procurator fiscal stood up.

'Now sir, is your name Joe Bloggs?'

'Yes, that's right.'

'Do you reside at 11 Cherrytree Avenue?'

'No, I stay at 1 Beechgrove Gardens.'

'Oh, a change of address. Now Mr Bloggs, on the 11th November, were you in the Dog and Duck Public House having a drink.'

'No sir, I wasn't,' replied a puzzled Joe Bloggs.

The sheriff stared at the procurator fiscal, who carried on with his questions.

'Is it true that you witnessed an assault which took place in the Dog and Duck Public House that evening?'

'No sir,' replied Mr Bloggs.

'Mr Fiscal,' said the sheriff, 'what is going on here?'

'I'll have this little problem cleared in a minute M'lord,' replied the procurator fiscal.

'Mr Bloggs, are you or are you not a witness in the case of an assault which occurred on 11th November within the Dog and Duck Public House?'

'I'm afraid not,' said Joe Bloggs.

'Well, what are you doing in the witness box?'

'Well,' said Joe Bloggs. 'I work for the Council and I'm here painting the hallway. I went in to the toilet and when I came out that man over there (pointing to the court usher) insisted that I came in here. I wanted to explain but he wouldn't let me.'

COLD ENOUGH TO FREEZE

One winter night, when the temperature was well below freezing, an old sergeant stationed at Oxgangs police station in Edinburgh, boasted of how his Skoda could start in any conditions. His Skoda was designed to survive the winters of Eastern Europe and so a Scottish winter could have no effect on it.

It was with a surprised expression that he returned to the station at the end of the nightshift. He was amazed, 'It's so cold the wheels have frozen to the ground!' he exclaimed.

He was totally embarrassed when a member of the dayshift removed the bricks from the front and rear of the Skoda's wheels.

Victoria age 6

THE CASE OF THE MISSING RADIO

A young man was accused of stealing a radio from a house where he had been a guest at a party. The man was arrested a short while later, in a field near to the house. He was charged with the theft but the radio was not recovered.

Some months later the accused defended himself at the Sheriff Court. After the procurator fiscal had questioned the sergeant who had been one of the arresting officers, the accused seized his opportunity to quiz the experienced sergeant.

'You say I was at a party?'

'That's correct,' answered the sergeant calmly.

'You say I stole a radio?'

'That's correct.'

'You say you arrested me walking across a field?'

'That's correct.'

The young man's voice was getting louder as he became enraged at the sergeant's continued calmness and control.

'Was I carrying the radio at the time?' he shouted.

'No, you were not carrying the radio.'

'Well, what did I do with it then? Eh? Did I eat it?' the accused had lost all control by now.

'Are you asking me a question?' was the sergeant's reply.

'Aye, I am!'

The sergeant paused for a moment and then said, 'No, I don't think you did eat the radio.'

NEW BRAKES, AN OIL CHANGE AND AN MOT TEST

It was late one Saturday morning when I attended one of the most unusual calls I ever received.

I was working in the Stockbridge area of Edinburgh and I had several calls already to attend to. Then the message came over my radio, 'A 999 call – attend at . . . , where a home help has discovered an old lady in a distressed condition.'

Normally this would mean that an old lady had been found lying with a broken leg or in urgent need of medical care.

I put my other calls to the side for the time being and made my way to the address of the old lady. When I entered the house I was met by the home help who was calmly going about her chores.

'Where's the old lady and what's wrong with her?' I asked.

'She's in there,' replied the home help, pointing to the livingroom whilst doing her dusting at the same time.

I remember thinking to myself, 'How callous can you be? She's not even helping the old woman.'

I entered the living room expecting to find an old lady lying on the floor, but instead she was sitting in her wheelchair with a tartan shawl round her legs.

'Come in son,' she told me, with a cheery grin on her rosy-cheeked face.

'Em, I received a call that eh, that you were in some sort of trouble,' I said.

'That's right, son,' she nodded.

'What is the problem?' I then asked her.

'It's my wheelchair son. The brakes aren't working right' she replied, pointing down to the mechanism on the right hand side of her chair.

I could see what was wrong right away. A little nut and bolt had fallen off. I replaced it and tightened it up.

'Thanks very much, son' she said as she tested the mechanism, just to make sure I had done the job properly. 'Would you like a cup of tea now?'

'No, thank you, I'm very busy,' I told her and headed off to attend to my many other calls.

Another message came across my radio, 'What was the result to the 999 call about the old lady in distress?'

'New brakes, an oil change and an MOT test,' I retorted.

'What?' called a puzzled controller.

'I'll explain when I get in.'

Grant Menzies age 7

NEW YEAR'S DAY REQUEST

It was New Year's Day, about 6.30pm and I was very busy. I had just attended to a call and had got back into the panda car. I made some notes in my notebook and then I heard a knock on the door window. I looked up and saw a young man obviously wishing to speak to me. I rolled down the window and said, 'Can I help you?'

'Any chance of a lift?' was the reply.

'I'm sorry,' I told him. 'But I'm very busy. There's a taxi rank over there though.'

'No, no,' he said shaking his head. 'I meant any chance of getting lifted?'

'You mean you want me to arrest you,' I asked, puzzled at his request.

'Aye, arrest me and lock me up.'

He had obviously been drinking but he wasn't really drunk. I told him I couldn't arrest him but I was curious to hear why he wanted to be arrested.

'Do you not recognise me?' he asked.

I stared at him and then realised that we had been at secondary school together. I nodded my head and said, 'Yes.'

'I'm an alcoholic. I've lost my job and I'm no use to anyone. Could you not just lock me up?'

He was only twenty-five years old, it was New Year's Day, a day when most people celebrate and I was being asked by a former school colleague to 'Lock him up'.

I asked him where he stayed. It was only a hundred yards along the road. I persuaded him to go home to his family, reassuring him that they wouldn't view him in such a poor light as he did himself.

Before going, I gave him an address and telephone number where he could seek help for his drinking problem.

He thanked me and wished me a 'Happy New Year'.

I later heard that he had taken my advice and sought help for his problem.

Sometimes all you can do to help someone is give them advice and reassurance. It may not seem a lot, but at least it's something.

BEAT

NO CRIB FOR A BED

Mike was a beat man in one of the rougher areas of the city. There was high unemployment and a high crime rate as well as the usual social problems that go hand in hand with unemployment. Needless to say, police officers weren't always popular with certain sectors of the community.

Mike, however, was the exception to the rule. Everyone in the community respected him and many saw him as more than a police officer. They looked upon him as a social worker and marriage guidance counsellor and one winter's morning his medical skills were put to the test by one of them.

Mike was working nightshift and had just returned to the box to make a note in the log book. As he entered the time in the book, 1.30am, he heard a knock on the door. He looked out of the window but could not see anyone. Then he opened the door and checked outside. There, huddled against the wall at the side of the box, he saw a young teenage girl. He recognised her immediately. She came from one of the problem families on his beat. The father drank, the mother drank, they argued and fought and she would frequently run away from it all.

Mike asked her why she was out at that time of the morning, in the freezing cold and not even wearing a coat. She didn't answer but just stared at the ground.

'Problems at home?' he continued, as he put his coat around her shoulders. She shook her head.

'No.'

'Well, what is it then?'

She kept staring at the ground.

'I . . . , I'm going to have a baby,' she told him in a quiet voice, the tears now running down her cheeks.

Mike stood back and looked at her. She was wearing a baggy jumper and as she was only a slip of a girl, it was difficult to see if she was telling the truth.

She looked up at him and straightaway Mike knew that she was telling him the truth. Then she doubled over in pain.

'She's going into labour,' thought Mike, as he helped her into the box, reassuring her that everything would be alright (it was actually Mike that required the reassuring).

He picked up the telephone to call his station, but before the operator answered, her waters broke. Mike dropped the telephone receiver to attend to his patient. And so at 2.15am he delivered a baby boy of six and half pounds in the confines of a police box.

There seemed to be something biblical about the whole thing.

Mike removed his two woollen jumpers and used them, together with a clean towel, to wrap the child in.

'Mike, Mike, are you alright,' sounded from the dangling telephone receiver.

Mike picked it up with his right hand whilst cradling the newborn with his left.

'Never been better,' he said. 'Send a car quickly.' And he gave a reassuring smile to the young mother.

Grant Menzies age 7

LOOKING AFTER THE OLD FOLK

Willie was the epitome of the community bobby and I would have to say I was proud and privileged to have worked with him.

He had a great affection for the old folk on his beat and always took time to visit the Old Folks' Centre and have a chat with them there. There was also some sheltered housing on his beat and he was well known amongst the residents for his daily calls, just to make sure they were alright and to brighten up their day.

It was about 11am one Friday and we had cleared all our paperwork and attended all our calls.

'It's pretty quiet now,' said Willie, 'Let's go and see old Mrs Brown,' and he strode off towards the sheltered housing complex, bidding a 'Good morning' to all he met on the way.

When we arrived at the house, Willie knocked at the door and it was opened by a grey haired little woman, whose face beamed with delight on seeing who was there.

'Come in Willie, it's nice to see you. I'll just put the kettle on,' she chirped. 'Oh, you've got a youngster with you today.'

We went inside and sat down and waited for the kettle to boil. Willie asked her how she was keeping and whether she required any help with anything. Messages, house repairs, whatever. Then he asked her if she had got herself a safety chain for her door.

'Aye,' she replied.

'And where is it?' asked Willie. 'You'll need to put it on the door.'

'I tried, but I couldn't manage it, what with me having arthritis in my hands,' she sighed.

'Where is it?' Willie asked.

'In the drawer,' she replied, pointing to the sideboard in the livingroom.

'Do you have a screwdriver?'

'It's in the same drawer, Willie.'

Up jumped Willie from his seat and off came his jacket. The sleeves were rolled up and the next thing you know, he had fitted the safety chain to the door.

'There you are,' smiled Willie. 'It's a lot more use there than it was sitting in the drawer.'

'That's awfully good of you, Willie,' she replied with a smile reminiscent to that of a child's on Christmas morning.

'That's what we're here for Mrs Brown. Now what about that cup of tea.'

A cup of tea and a chat later and we headed off to patrol more of the beat. Through the small gap in the doorway, caused by her new safety chain restricting its opening, Mrs Brown smiled and waved to us.

'Cheerio Willie, cheerio son,' she called as we went on our way.

As we walked down the road Willie turned to me and with a 'now listen to my advice' look on his face, told me, 'We've got to look after the old folk. After all we might be lucky enough to reach that age ourselves one day.'

ON REFLECTION

A youth made off from a stolen car which he abandoned in the Braid Hills area of Edinburgh. Officers surrounded the area as it was known that the youth had gone to ground in some undergrowth on the bank of a hill.

A constable, who had a high vantage point, was able to see the youth lying in the grass. By means of his radio the constable signalled that the youth was approximately ten yards in front of the police motorcyclist, wearing a white helmet.

The youth was arrested a short while later but not before it was realised that there was no police motorcyclist and that what the constable had seen was the reflection of the sun on an old sergeant's bald head!

JACK OF ALL TRADES

Three o'clock in the morning. The boys in blue refer to this as 'the death hour'. Statistically it is the time for sudden deaths. So when the code '10' call crackled through the radio I concluded the worst.

'Panda Charlie attending, over and out.' Well that's me for the night I groaned to myself. I swung the panda violently around the next corner on the left and rehearsed in my mind the standard procedure for dealing with sudden deaths. Probably the auld man. The controller had said the caller was a neighbour of the 'wifie up the stair'.

Always the top flat. This street was full of 'auld wifies'. Most of them were born here – married here – raised a family here – no doubt they would die there too!

The wee wifie across the landing came out to greet me. From her toothless face a garbled, incoherent account of the problem generated. She shuffled in her oversized slippers towards the door of 'auld Maggie Jones', her tent-like nightdress flowing behind her and her shoulders mantled in the ceremonial Glasgow wifie's shawl. Her short stature meant she did not have to stoop to insert the standard check key which fitted every door in the stair.

'Haw Maggie, it's the polis.' assaulted my ears. With this I was heralded into the 'but and bed' abode. The turned down gas mantle cast an eerie glow in the over furnished room. This was the kitchen, clean in every corner – the deal table scrubbed white with a silk runner across from corner to corner.

From the hole-in-the-wall bed, a high-pitched voice filled the room. Maggie was propped up with pillows, wearing the customary granny shawl, like her neighbour.

'It's that tap,' Maggie wailed, having first taken time to insert her falsies from the mug on her bedside table. Water still dribbled from her mouth as she continued.

'It's been drippin' aw night, cannae git ony sleep at a',' she continued to adjust her teeth in her mouth as she spoke.

All this had been conducted in virtual silence on my part. My audience now waited for my contribution to the situation. The auld Glasgow bobby was held in reverence by senior citizens – he knew everything – he was the panacea for all ills!

'I'll see what I can do, Granny' I promised as I walked towards the sink under the window.

The swan-neck well dropped a continuous drip of water into the white enamelled basin beneath, setting up a rhythmic beat which even Louis Armstrong might have been proud of. This was the cause of Granny's insomnia.

'Needs a new washer' I announced in an official type manner after trying to tighten the handle to no avail. 'Need to get the landlord in, in the morning.'

I was about to make exit stage left but was prevented by the toothless neighbour, who surveyed me with folded arms and a defiant look which said, 'You're not getting off *that* easy.'

'Landlord?' cried Granny. 'Oor landlord takes ages tae dae onything – widnae gee ye daylight in a dark corner.'

I was concerned. Looking about for inspiration I spied a fine array of medicine bottles which might have out-numbered that in any chemist's shop.

'Granny, do you use this medicine any more?' I asked lifting one which contained a red coloured liquid labelled 'The Mixture'. I was more interested in the cork at the top.

'Naw constable, nane o' thay things dae me any guid at ma age.'

Emptying The Mixture into the sink, I stuffed the cork into the end of the swan neck. A little tap into place with the baton – silence.

'That's it Granny, but get the plumber to fix a new washer soon. Have a good night's sleep.'

The toothless neighbour escorted me to the door and despatched me with some more incoherent words. I think she was smiling, so perhaps they were thank you's?

Three weeks later when reporting for a back shift, word was left for me to report right away to the superintendent. This usually meant trouble.

'Stand easy Davie' he said as I stood to attention behind his desk. 'I've a letter here passed down from the Chief Constable's Office.'

'It gets worse,' I thought.

'It's something about an early morning plumbing job . . . !'

PANDA CHARLIE

'Panda Charlie, Panda Charlie, come in Panda Charlie,' the radio boomed in my ear. These new extension speakers for the car certainly worked well, too well sometimes.

I reacted instinctively to the call sign, automatically pulling into a nearby bus bay. At this time in the morning, 2am, it was quiet, a bit too quiet! 'Panda Charlie receiving, over.'

No reply, were they receiving me? I lifted the radio out of the car receiver unit and stepped outside to send another signal, hopefully more successfully. My stepping out of the car coincided with the noise of a thud, dull thump, regular thump, stop, then another blow. Somewhere something unusual was happening.

'Panda Charlie to control, are you receiving me?' I tried again.

'Crackle . . . crackle . . . !'

'Panda Charlie to control, if you're receiving this signal please note I'm investigating a thumping noise near number 723 Duncan Place, over and out.'

The responding 'crackle, crackle,' suggested that perhaps they had received the signal from me.

I thought of the radio controller in his warm office at the station as the icy cold blast struck my face. I adjusted my cap, pulled my collar up and checked the baton strap was handy. Could be anything!

As I locked the panda car, I said to myself, 'So much for the new radio system,' and moved towards the thumping sound.

My ear directed me up the three flights of stairs. My attention was drawn to the centre door which was lying open. The noise of hammering had stopped now. Had they seen me?

I checked myself at the wooden doorbar to catch my breath. The brass monkey on the doorknocker seemed to expand and contract with each breath. Must be out of condition. I made a mental note to restart my physical exercises.

As the last of the three official type knocks died away a little man appeared carrying a claw hammer. I tightened the grip on my baton strap. Aren't we such a suspicious lot, us cops?

His first words took me by surprise.

'Blo . . . h . . . that was quick.'

'What do you mean, sir?' I asked, trying to sound official.

'Am jist aff the phone the noo' replied the wee man. You learn to be quick thinking and inventive in this job.

'Aye man it's one of the wonders of modern technology, the short wave interconnected base to field radio.' The look on the little man's face was priceless. I had completely bamboozled him.

His mouth was still hanging open when I asked him, 'What seems to be the trouble anyway, sir?'

'Ach, it's a burst pipe as usual, these auld hooses are a' the same. Time they were pulled doon!' he complained as he led me to the source of the trouble.

I dwarfed the little man as I followed behind him. He was wearing striped pyjamas. His bald head and grey side locks gave his age away. It was as well I put on my heavy boots, we were now wading through water.

'Av bashed maist o' the pipe flat, but there's still a trickle o' water, a'll need tae git it aff?' he wailed. 'The woman doon the stair is moanin' her heid aff.'

'Panda Charlie to control.' I tried again.

'Crackle . . . crackle . . .'

'Please send me the Water Board to number 723 Duncan Place, top flat, middle door, over and out.'

'That's it sir, they'll be here shortly.'

The wee man looked towards the door as though expecting them to appear any minute.

I left the water logged area post haste and descended the three flights of stairs in a fraction of the time I had taken to ascend them.

The occasion called for the use of Alexander Graham Bell's proven telecommunication system. I used the 'Doctor Who' box and learned that 723 Duncan Place had been the subject of the last call. Wonderful things these short wave interconnected base to field radios, I smiled to myself.

'Panda Charlie, calling Panda Charlie, come in please.'

THE PHANTOM PIANIST OF OLD EDINBURGH TOWN

Nightshift in the city of Edinburgh was quite fascinating. The moods of the city at night were quite tangible. On the quiet of a summer's night the zephyrs of wind would catch the cords on flagpoles, high up on the solid grey buildings.

To the night duty policeman, with little experience, it was the nearest sound you could get to a hacksaw cutting through the bars of some jeweller's shop on your beat. You could hear, in the distance, the sound of locomotives shunting up at the railway station and smell the faint aroma of the breweries on the breeze. The stillness was profound in the streets and lanes that interlaced the main blocks of the substantial stone buildings.

In one of the lanes a bric-a-brac sale was held twice a week. They would auction off pots and pans, garden tools, gas stoves, lamps, furniture and old pianos. What wasn't sold lay about for a few days to be later removed or broken up.

On one particular misty night a piano stood in the lane. It was old and pitiful looking, but it attracted the beat man as he strolled down the lane checking the property.

He stood and admired it as it obviously had at one time been a work of art. Then with his torchlight shining on windows and doors, he continued on down the lane to the exit at the other end.

As he turned the corner he heard a faint tinkling sound of piano keys. He stopped and listened carefully.

'Must have imagined it,' he said to himself.

Then he heard it again. It was piano keys being played. He retraced his steps and carefully looked round the corner into the lane. There was no one there. Just the old piano. He walked along and had another look at it.

'Maybe a rat had ran across the keys or it had moved slightly on its castors causing the keys to rattle,' he thought.

He made his way back down the lane and out into the street. Then he heard it again. It was definitely the piano, only this time it was a recognisable tune that was being played.

He took to his heels and ran back into the lane. Not a soul in sight. Just the old piano and some other discarded bric-a-brac.

Puffing and panting, he checked the piano once more. It hadn't been moved and a few rattles on the top of it with his fist did not produce any rodent from it. Anyway, no rat or mouse could have played the tune that he had heard coming from it.

There were no signs whatsoever of anyone else having been in the lane. Suddenly the hair was prickling at the back of his neck as he came to the conclusion that he was experiencing something out of the unknown.

Very quietly he made his way out of the lane and back to the station.

He took off his jacket and went into the mess room. He sat down at the table and stared into space, still trying to come to terms with his experience.

'What's wrong with you tonight?' asked one of his colleagues, who obviously noticed a difference in his character. 'You look as if you've seen a ghost.'

He didn't answer. How could he explain to them without appearing foolish?

His lack of response caused the others to stop their game of cards and find out what was wrong with their normally jovial colleague.

After much persuasion, he decided to tell them.

'And that's the truth, lads' he said to them at the end of his tale.

Not one word of scorn was said in reply as all were aware of the tales of the supernatural in which the city is steeped. But one of the officers broke the silence. He knew that there was a logical explanation for the occurrence.

He had also been out patrolling the area and on hearing his colleague enter the lane, he had followed on to have a chat with him. Seeing the piano he played a few bars and then decided to have a bit of fun and hid from view when his colleague returned to check it out.

There was no Phantom Pianist of Old Edinburgh Town, only a mischievous colleague.

Grant Menzies age 7

WELCOME TO PORKY'S!!

'Sarge you must see the size of the pigs at Gogar,' a young officer pleaded at the Mess Room table of a police station in Edinburgh.

It was the early hours of a summer's morning when the excited constable finally persuaded his sergeant to go along with him to the pig farm at Gogar. The sun had not yet started to rise and the experienced sergeant chose his footing carefully while his junior rushed onward, bursting with enthusiasm.

Suddenly the younger of the two officers disappeared. After the longest two seconds of his life he re-emerged from the open cesspit and dragged himself to firmer ground, spitting and snorting.

He was very embarrassed at being made to travel back to the station in the open boot of the panda car. He was even more embarrassed when he had to stand in the front car park of the police station while he was hosed down. Early morning shift workers appeared to be very puzzled by the picture.

Mark Menzies age 9

ONE OF THE OLD SCHOOL

'Bravo one-five to Bravo, I have found the missing youth sleeping rough in the old graveyard. I'll bring him into the station if you would contact the parents for me'.

That was the message I received from one of the car men when I was working in the control room of my station.

A few minutes later, into the station walked Jimmy and with him a young lad about thirteen or fourteen years of age.

Jimmy was one of the older constables on the shift. He knew the ins and outs of the job and a few shortcuts as well. He stood about six feet tall and his years of fitness and weight training were obvious. His greying hair and weathered looks gave away his years, otherwise he was as fit and as strong as a man half his years.

I couldn't help comparing him in my mind to Bumper Morgan, the character in the film The Blue Knight, which was about a hardened, streetwise, American cop.

As he walked into the control room, he pulled over a chair and said to the young lad, 'There y'are son, have a seat'.

The lad was pale and tired looking. He was wearing jeans and a jumper and carried an old quilted blanket. His face was grubby looking and his hair was in need of a brush and comb.

'I found him sleeping rough in the old graveyard', Jimmy told us. 'Had a row with his parents and ran away. He doesn't even have any money, just that old blanket'.

As we waited for the arrival of his parents, I noticed the colour coming back into his cheeks as he enjoyed the warmth of the control room. Then, from beneath his blanket he pulled out a sealed packet of sandwiches (the type you can buy in snack-bars and 24-hour service stations). As he opened the packet and began to eat them, I turned to Jimmy and asked, 'If he had no money, how did he get the sandwiches?'

The hard outer shell began to crack and a shade of redness glowed through Jimmy's well tanned face as he replied, 'I bought them for him'.

'You're just as soft as anyone else under that hard outer shell', I told him as we both smiled, Jimmy in embarrassment, myself in admiration.

'One of the old school son', said Jimmy, as he pulled out his spectacles and put them on before writing out his report on the matter.

REVENGE

It was during the early hours of the morning when two beat men heard the sound of breaking glass. They set off and ran in the direction of the sound and when they were near a newsagent's shop, they saw a youth jumping out of the window and running off. He ran through the back gardens of houses and tenement blocks and down the back alleys.

One of the officers, being 6' 5" tall, disturbed sleeping pigeons whilst running through a narrow close, before arresting the youth by means of a text book rugby tackle.

Two days later, about 10am, the same two officers were walking along the street where the chase had ended.

As they chatted away, the taller one suddenly found that his hat and tunic were decorated with white matter.

Looking up to the roofs above, he saw the 'artist', one of the pigeons he had disturbed during the chase.

His colleague smiled.

'Revenge is sweet' he said.

'That's a matter of opinion' replied his colleague, wiping the pigeon droppings from his hat.

RUGBY TACKLE

During the British tour of the South African Springboks Rugby Team in the 1970's, many of their games were disrupted by anti-apartheid demonstrators.

Police officers from all over were drafted in to assist at matches taking place at Murrayfield in Edinburgh and at Galashiels in the Border Region.

At the Galashiels game, a group of officers were assigned to line the route to the turnstiles of the ground, to protect spectators from the threats of the somewhat hostile crowd.

As the spectators lined up waiting to get into the game, one demonstrator tried to hand out leaflets to them but was stopped from doing so by the police to prevent any conflict taking place.

Not pleased at the action of the police, the demonstrator approached a sergeant and began to complain to him.

The sergeant explained the reason behind the police action and the somewhat frustrated demonstrator changed his line of attack.

'Sergeant, I believe that there are two men standing behind the police van smoking cigarettes. Isn't that against your discipline code?'

The sergeant was just about to explain to the man that they had been given permission to have a break and therefore were entitled to have a cigarette during that time. However, he was saved the trouble of explaining.

A wee wifie sporting a Galashiels Rugby Club scarf, burst out of the queue of spectators and walloped the man across the backside with her umbrella saying,

'Ya dirty midden. Ah'll teach you to grass on the polis.'

Whereupon the man took to his heels never to be seen again.

The woman was given a stern word in her ear before entering the ground to a great cheer from the rest of the spectators.

PERHAPS THE MOST DIFFICULT JOB

It was about a week, maybe two, before Christmas Day. I was working nightshift and that particular night there were only two of us on duty at the station.

About 2am we were having our break and were sitting having a game of cards in the canteen, when we received a radio message asking us to phone the control room.

My colleague did this and was informed that we had to attend at a house and deliver a death message, perhaps the most difficult job a police officer can undertake.

It turned out that we had to call on a woman and inform her that her husband, who had been ill in hospital for a couple of weeks, had died there.

We put on our hats and tunics and made our way down to the house.

There was a lengthy wait after knocking on the door, then a light went on and it was opened. Behind it stood a lad in his late teens.

'Is your mother in?' asked my colleague.

'Aye, do you want to see her?' replied the youth.

'If you don't mind, son.'

'I'll go and wake her up. Just come in.'

The young lad showed us into the livingroom and then went upstairs to waken his mother.

It was while we were waiting in the livingroom that the full unpleasantness of our task began to sink in. In one corner of the room was the Christmas tree, decorated appropriately. Some of the decorations were bought from a shop and some obviously made by children, perhaps at school.

Running through both our minds was the question, 'Are there young children in the family?'

Our suspicions were confirmed when we saw items of clothing and several pairs of shoes which obviously belonged to children.

Then the mother came into the livingroom. She was no more than forty years old, but looked like a woman approaching retirement. Her frail figure and drawn features were the signs of many months, maybe years, of worry.

'What's wrong?' she asked, her voice trembling knowing that only bad news is conveyed by the police at that time of the morning.

After confirming that she was the wife of the man who had died, my colleague continued speaking.

'I'm afraid I've got some bad news for you. It's about your husband,' he said in a soft and sympathetic voice.

'Is he, has he got worse?' she asked.

My colleague slowly shook his head from side to side, 'I'm afraid.'

He didn't have to say anymore. In fact he didn't, maybe couldn't.

She nodded in acknowledgement and asked, 'What time?' as she lowered herself slowly into the armchair.

'About an hour ago,' my colleague told her, his voice now a whisper.

Meanwhile, I was stunned into silence. I couldn't help wondering about her young family. How this shouldn't happen to anyone at Christmas time.

She called in her eldest son and told him the bad news. We asked her if we could do anything for her – inform relatives or take her to the hospital. She politely declined the offer saying that she would contact her brother-in-law and he would take her.

We could see that she now wanted to be on her own and we respected her silent wish.

We found out from staff at the hospital that the woman knew that her husband's death was imminent. Yet, even when the time came she had clung to the hope that we were there to tell her that his condition had worsened, before submitting to the truth.

No matter how much someone is expecting this sort of news, they are never totally prepared for it. And we will never be able to make it any easier for them to receive.

SEALED WITH A KISS

The sergeant called one of his beat constables into his office.

'Tom, come in and have a seat.'

The constable sat down.

'What's the problem, sarge?'

'It's one of the old women on your beat. We've had a representative from the Gas Board on the phone to us about her. They've been out several times this week to check her house for a gas leak. She's complaining that her neighbours below are pumping gas into her house through the floorboards. They've checked it out just in case, but there are no leaks. I've been in touch with the Social Work Department, who say they'll give her a visit, but how about going round yourself and having a talk with her?'

'Yes, sure sarge,' replied Tom.

So Tom went round to see the old lady, but before doing so he picked up a roll of masking tape from the stationery cupboard.

He went round to the old lady's house and over a cup of tea, he heard all about the gas being pumped up through the floorboards.

Tom nodded sympathetically during the conversation and afterwards he put down his tea-cup and took out the roll of masking tape.

'Now, dear,' he said. 'I've been speaking to the experts about this and this is what they gave me.'

'What is it?' asked the old lady.

'It's special tape,' replied Tom. 'It prevents poisonous gases coming through floorboards.'

Then he proceeded to put the tape round the skirting board of the livingroom.

'There you are. That's your house perfectly safe from the gas. You can sleep safely at night now.'

The old lady thanked him with a kiss on the cheek and he went on his way.

Every now and again he would call in to make sure everything was alright and, if necessary, renew any pieces of masking tape which had come loose.

SIGN HERE PLEASE

The venue was the Usher Hall in Edinburgh. The occasion was one of the early concerts of the Peter Pan of the pop world, Cliff Richard.

A sergeant and team of constables were assigned to the concert to take care of the crowds of young women who were desperate to catch a glimpse of their idol after the concert.

As expected, the crowd assembled outside the main doors of the concert hall and began to chant, 'We want Cliff, we want Cliff.'

What they didn't realise was that Cliff was long gone, having escaped through the side door of the building.

The sergeant in charge appeared and managed to gain silence for a few moments, during which time he tried to explain to the crowd that Cliff had gone. The women wouldn't buy it and one of them called out, 'We're staying until we get his autograph.'

Then they began to chant once more, 'We want Cliff, we want Cliff.'

The sergeant went inside the building and then re-appeared a few minutes later.

'Can I have your attention please?' he called to the women. 'Mr Richard has agreed to take your autograph books and photographs and sign them on the condition that you all leave afterwards. Unfortunately he cannot come out to see you.'

After a short discussion the women agreed to the terms and handed over their books and photographs to the sergeant. The sergeant then called over six of his men and went inside the building once more.

'Right lads,' he said to them. 'Start signing – Best Wishes, Cliff. And eh, add a few kisses as well.'

So there they were, signing the books and photographs and then returning them to the women, who left quite contented.

Just as well they didn't stop to compare signatures!!

A SONG FROM JOHN

I remember the day one of my old sergeants retired. It was a bright summer's morning and I was walking along the main street through the town when I met a man, who for the purpose of my story, I will call John.

John was in his fifties and was mentally handicapped. He was a cheery character and loved to chat to the local police. He would regularly come in to the station or wave down the panda car so that he could sing his latest song to you.

His other passion was collecting empty lemonade bottles, with which he could earn 10p for each one he returned to the corner shop.

'Morning, John,' I said to him.

'Hiya. Are there any bottles in the station?' he asked.

'I don't know. Come along and we'll have a look.'

So we strolled along the street to the station.

'Do you know that the sergeant is retiring today?' I asked John.

'No. What does that mean?'

I explained to him that he had been in the police for thirty years and this was his last day.

'Oh,' said John. 'Will I sing a song to him?'

'If you want to' I replied.

'What will I sing?'

'Anything you want, John. I'm sure he will like it.'

We went into the station and the sergeant was just putting on the kettle for the morning tea break.

'Hello, John,' said the sergeant.

'Sit down sarge. John has a surprise for you.' I told him.

The sergeant sat down and I gave John the nod.

'Happy Birthday to you, Happy Birthday to you' sang John, right to the very end.

The sergeant's eyes filled with tears and he found difficulty in speaking for a few seconds. John was so pleased with himself. He didn't understand what a retirement meant, but he knew that it was a special occaion. Just like a birthday.

The sergeant fought back the tears.

'That was lovely, John. Would you like a cup of tea?'

'No thanks.'

'What about a doughnut?'

'Oh aye. I like doughnuts.'

So John got a doughnut and a couple of empty lemonade bottles and went on his way, quite happy with himself.

'Well' said the sergeant. 'I just know now that my last day is going to be a good one.'

And so it was. But that's another story.

Frances Ann Moneghan

STRIKING UP A BARGAIN

A man appeared at the court to explain to the sheriff why he had not been paying his fine. The sheriff peered down at the man and sternly said, 'The last time you appeared in front of me you agreed to pay your fine in instalments of £2 per week. So far you have only made the payment once and you are a long way behind with the other payments. I would like to know what your excuse is.'

The man swallowed a couple of times before beginning his answer.

'Well you see, eh,' he said nervously. 'I've had a lot of problems at home.'

'Have you?' said the sheriff. 'And what exactly were they and why did they prevent you from paying your fine?'

Bowing his head he told the sheriff.

'Well sir, my wife left me and I started drinking a lot and spent all my money on drink.'

Then raising his head with a small amount of pride he stated, 'But I've been getting help for my drink problem and I've stopped again.'

'Very well,' said the sheriff. 'Now maybe you will agree to pay your fine and save me the bother of sending you to jail.'

'I will, sir. It's just that I find £2 per week a bit much to cope with right now.'

'Would you like to suggest an alternative rate of payment?' the sheriff asked him.

The man thought long and hard, then looking pleased with himself he asked, 'How about £4 per fortnight?'

The sheriff shook his head in disbelief. 'Make it £1 per week,' he told the sheriff clerk. 'Next case please.'

THE ROBBER WHO GOT 'MUG-GED'

A police constable received a radio message to attend at a small gift shop where a member of staff wished to report an incident.

When he arrived he spoke to the young shop assistant who nonchalantly informed him that a man had tried to rob the shop.

After establishing that no one had been hurt, the constable asked the shop assistant for a description of the man. She was very vague with her description and informed the constable that the incident had taken place over thirty minutes ago.

After circulating the description of the man to other officers by radio, the constable asked the young woman to give a statement to him.

'Oh very well,' she said, 'It wasn't much of an affair, but I thought I better report it anyway. About 1.30 I was serving a customer and there were several others waiting to be served, when this drunk little man came into the shop. He was carrying an empty wine bottle and he came right up to the counter. I told him that he would have to wait in the queue and then he said to me, "This is a robbery. Give me your money", and he waved the bottle in the air.'

'I told him that he was drunk and not to be so stupid. Then he said the same thing to me.'

'What did you do this time?' asked the constable.

'Well, it was becoming very embarrassing so I said "I've got customers to serve, now please leave the shop," but he just ignored my request. Then he said to me, "I'm not joking. This is a robbery." '

'What happened after this?' enquired the constable.

'Well, I'm afraid I lost my temper and was quite rude. I said to him, "I'm very busy. Now p..s off you drunken little man!" '

'What reaction did he give when you said that to him?'

'Not a lot. He just stood there a bit stunned looking and stared all around the shop. Then he picked up a coffee mug and asked how much it cost. I told him £1 and he reached into his pocket and threw a pound note on to the counter before running out of the shop. As I said before it wasn't much of an affair.'

THE MEETING

I remember one day when I had been cited to attend at court. My normal duty that day should have been a 2pm–10pm backshift, but because of the court case my hours were changed to a 10am–6pm dayshift.

I arrived at the court at 10am and by 11am I was free to go as the case had been adjourned. It was a lovely summer day and since my shift team would not be on until 2pm, and I knew I was marked on the duty sheets as 'attending court', I decided to take an extended lunch break and go and play a few holes of golf before returning to the station. I jumped into my car and headed off to the course.

I decided to play the first six holes and then cut across the course and play the 17th and 18th holes, finishing at the clubhouse. This I did but on reaching the 18th tee, I saw a man about to play the hole, so I stood back and waited.

After he had played his shot he noticed me waiting and invited me to join him for the last hole. I thanked him and hit my tee shot. Quite a nice drive if I say so myself. Straight down the middle.

As we walked down the fairway we chatted to each other. Then he asked me if I was on holiday. I told him that I wasn't and that I had been at the court. Then I thought I should explain. I told him that I was a police officer and that the court case had been adjourned, so I decided to play a few holes of golf before returning to my station.

'And what division do you work in?' he then asked me.

I told him which division it was and explained that I worked from the sub-divisional station and not the divisional headquarters.

'That would explain why you don't recognise me,' he said, nodding his head.

'I'm sorry, I can't say I do.'

'I'm the chief inspector at your divisional headquarters,' he said, looking like the cat that got the canary.

I was left speechless and needless to say I didn't play very well for the rest of that hole.

WAITING FOR THE END

One of the most unpleasant jobs a police officer has to carry out is dealing with a sudden death. One of the aspects that you never forget is the pungent smell of a corpse.

I remember one hot summer's morning, I was patrolling a small town beat with an older constable. As we made our way along the street we were approached by a milkman. He informed us that he had just placed two bottles of milk at the door of an elderly woman who stayed on the first floor of a block of flats and was concerned for her safety. He told us that her door was ajar and that there was a strange smell coming from within.

My colleague and I feared the worst. We went up to the house and went inside. The smell was definitely similar to the one associated with a sudden death. We checked the livingroom but it was empty.

As we approached the kitchen we could feel a tremendous heat coming from it. When we opened the door, we saw the old woman sitting in front of an electric fire, which was on full. Her eyes were closed but they opened when we spoke to her. Not wishing to alarm her, we told her that we were just passing and saw her milk on the doorstep and decided to take it in for her.

She thanked us and told us that she was waiting for her daughter to visit her. We asked if she was well and whether we could get anything for her. She told us that she was fine and requested a drink of water. The heat in the kitchen was incredible, but she did not wish the fire to be turned off.

We said goodbye and went on our way but we both couldn't help thinking that we would be called back in the near future.

Two days later we were. We were met by the old lady's doctor who informed us that she had died. He told us that he would grant the death certificate as she had been terminally ill and he had been treating her.

I felt so sad for the old lady. That day we had visited her, she must have known that the end was near and yet all she wished for was a glass of water and the comfort of her electric fire.

THE HAND THAT FEEDS HIM

Two detective officers, approaching the end of their service, reminisced over their early days. One related the story of the first domestic dispute he attended.

'We were talking to the wife in the kitchen of the house while the husband held the family pet alsation in the living room. The dog was vicious and had barked from the time we entered the house.

Suddenly the wife left the kitchen and the argument started up again in the living room. Before we could follow the wife, the alsation entered the kitchen, snarling and growling. It caused us to back off into the kitchen.

Quick as a flash my tutor grabbed a pan of mince from the stove and put it on the floor in front of the dog. The dog scoffed the lot in seconds and my tutor returned to pan to the stove.

We walked through to the living room and to the amazement of the feuding couple, the dog stood at my tutor's side and licked his hand. They were so surprised by the dog's change in nature that they stopped arguing and we left the house – matter resolved.'

Blair Davidson age 3

THE 'TAIL' OF TWO DOGS

About 1.30am on a bitterly, cold wet Sunday, the young probationer was plodding his way along through a mining area of a country town where he was stationed, when he heard the mournful howling of a dog. Thinking that the animal was in distress, and being a dog lover, he decided to investigate. He finally traced the animal, a young collie, and found it huddled against the front door of a dwelling house. The dog came bounding towards him, barking excitedly, then began cavorting to and from the dwelling house door.

Deciding that the occupants had inadvertently locked the dog out, the young officer knocked several times on the door with no response so, thinking that the inmates were in a comatose condition after a night on the bottle, he gave up and made to continue on his beat. The dog however had other ideas when it realised that it was being abandoned. It began to howl piteously then rose on its hind legs and tried to turn the door handle with its teeth. This display of canine intelligence so impressed the young officer that he returned to the dog's assistance and on turning the handle, found the door unlocked. Pushing it open, he let the dog in, then quietly closed it again before resuming his patrol.

The young officer had barely walked fifty yards when bedlam broke loose. On looking back he found the house in question now ablaze with lights and the profanity issuing from same simply appalling. Suddenly the front door opened and not one, but two dogs shot out and streaked up the road past him. The first dog was the young collie and the second appeared to be a black labrador. Chasing the dogs were two men in night attire – one was whistling loudly after the dogs, while the other was vowing vengeance on the idiot who had opened the house door. His maledictions suddenly ceased when the black labrador suddenly emerged from the darkness and obediently sat down at his feet. The behaviour of the two men changed instantaneously; one began to pet the dog while the other, looking upwards, thanked the Creator for its safe return.

Calm having been restored, the young officer allowed his curiosity to overcome his discretion by walking out of the shadows and requesting the cause of the disturbance.

The men explained that they were the owners of the black labrador – a bitch – which was the winner of many trophies. At present she was in season and being kept indoors during which time a young collie dog had been most persistent in his efforts to gain access to her. With rising anger they further stated that a few minutes previously some idiot had opened their front door and let this collie in with the result that, in the ensuing confusion, both dogs got out.

Realising that the valuable labrador bitch had come to no harm, our young officer decided to close the incident. Ignoring the desire of the men to wreak vengeance on the already mentioned idiot who was responsible for letting the offending collie dog into their house, he drew their attention to their condition. They were barefoot, trouserless and soaked to the skin, so he advised them to get indoors before catching a chill.

Still grumbling, the two men took his advice and once more he resumed his patrol, vowing that never gain would he allow a dog to lead him up the garden path to participate in an illegal entry.

TRY THIS SET FOR SIZE, SIR

The Grassmarket area in Edinburgh has regularly been associated with down and outs and winos.

Many years ago these unfortunate gents were often found lying drunk in the streets and subsequently were arrested and detained in custody, pending their appearance in court the next day.

Many of them sobered up enough to realise that they were no longer the owners of a set of false teeth. So, after they had been released from the court, they would head on down to the lost and found property office at the police station to report the loss. After they had done this the police officer there would produce a plastic bag containing a selection of false teeth, which were handed in as found property, whereupon the down and out would try various sets before finding one which best suited him!

WATER PUZZLE

A young constable found himself posted to a small village, which had a small police station with a police house next to it.

Each shift team at the station consisted of only two officers and the young constable was assigned to work with the seasoned constable who stayed at the police house next to the station. He was a jovial character whose hobby was deep-sea diving and he was a member of the police underwater rescue team.

After a few months had gone by, the senior constable told the younger one, 'I'm going to have a day off tomorrow, so it's up to you to look after things.'

'Don't worry,' replied the young constable, 'I won't let you down.'

The next day the young constable was sitting in the station doing some paper work when he began to hear a gurgling noise. Then it stopped. Then it started again. Then it stopped, then started. And so it continued.

Remembering his promise, he set about checking the radiators and the water pipes in the station. He could not find any leaks or faults so he decided to check the boiler room. Once more he could find nothing wrong but the noise definitely appeared to be coming from that area. Just to be safe he decided to call out the emergency plumber.

The plumber came out and checked the station thoroughly. 'It appears to be coming from next door,' he told the constable, 'I'd better check in there as well.'

So, the two of them went and knocked on the front door of the house. The wife of the senior constable opened the door and was informed of what was going on.

'Come in' she told them. 'My husband's in the bathroom. You'd better speak to him.'

As they made their way through the house to the bathroom, they could hear the gurgling noise. It was definitely coming from the bathroom.

They soon found out what was causing the noise and it was a case of red faces all around. For there in the bathtub, which was filled to the brim with water, was the senior constable, testing out his new snorkelling equipment!

CHRISTMAS 'TIME'

It was around the third week of December and two youths stood in the corridor of the Sheriff Court buildings, pondering over what the future held in store for them.

'Who's the sheriff in court today?' asked one of them.

'Don't worry' said the other. 'It's an old one who's quite lenient. In fact he's so kind when he gives out sentences he should be called Santa Claus.'

The trials began and the time came for the second youth to appear in the dock.

The sheriff clerk read out the charges which were assault, vandalism and breach of the peace.

'How do you plead?' he asked the youth.

'Eh, guilty to all of them,' replied the youth arrogantly and then proceeded to turn to his friend sitting in the courtroom and gave him a nod and a wink.

Now it was the turn of the sheriff to pass sentence on him. He cleared his throat and stared straight at the youth.

'Now then young man. This is not the first time that you have appeared before this court in answer to similar charges. This is a particularly nasty case which has been presented before me today and it will not be tolerated by this court.'

The youth gave another glance over to his mate and winked again.

The sheriff continued, 'You obviously have no respect for other people and their property and certainly none at all for law and order. I have no alternative but to sentence you to three month's imprisonment.'

The youth's arrogant smile soon disappeared as he stared at the sheriff in disbelief.

As two police officers led him from the courtroom the sheriff called out to him.

'Oh and by the way young man.' The youth turned round, obviously hoping that a reprieve was on its way.

'Merry Christmas.'

The youth left the courtroom puzzled as to whether the sheriff was being sincere with his seasonal greeting or had he overheard the conversation between him and his mate earlier that morning?

WRITTEN PROOF

The police motorcyclist signalled to the youth on the 50cc moped to pull into the side of the road and stop.

The officer got off from his motorcycle and spoke to the youth.

'You were speeding son. Forty two miles per hour in a built up area. The limit is thirty miles per hour.'

'I'm very sorry officer but I didn't think it would go that fast' replied the youth.

'I'll give you a warning this time but if you want to keep your licence clean I would advise you to slow down' the police officer told him.

'Are you not going to give me a ticket?' enquired the youth.

'We don't do that in this country. Take my advice and think yourself lucky you're getting a warning.'

'Could you give me a written warning?' asked the youth.

'Don't be silly son. Why on earth do you want a written warning?'

'I want to prove to my mates that I was stopped for speeding. They reckon my moped can't do over thirty and call it a sewing machine' said the dejected youth.

THE SIEGE

Saturday night and a sergeant and a constable were about to go out on a foot patrol in a small town, when they received a radio message.

'Foxtrot double two, could you attend at the chip shop in the main street where there is a doberman dog terrorising passers-by.'

The sergeant acknowledged the call and as he and the constable opened the front door of the station, they were confronted with the animal itself.

Beside the animal stood a rotund man (slightly the worse for drink) who was feeding it with chips from his fish supper.

'This is the dog that was trying to bite everyone,' he told the sergeant.

'Oh, well you'd better bring it inside,' replied the astonished sergeant.

The man led the dog through the public foyer into the station corridor.

'We'll put it in the kennel in the back yard,' the sergeant told the man. But when he tried to go near the dog it growled and snarled and showed him a full set of teeth.

'I don't think it wants to go,' laughed the man.

The sergeant agreed with him.

'Have you got any chips left?' the sergeant asked the man.

'Aye, do you want some?' he replied.

'Not for myself, for the dog,' the sergeant told him. 'Throw them into that interview room.'

So, the man threw some chips into the room and the dog followed on in. Once inside, the sergeant closed the door trapping it inside.

Once the man had left the station the sergeant and the constable returned to the muster room.

As the sergeant telephoned the control room to arrange for the dog to be uplifted, a CID officer arrived at the station. He entered the muster room and spoke to the other two officers on various matters.

As they chatted they heard a noise coming from the corridor. Then the door of the muster room slowly began to open.

To the horror of the three officers, through the gap in the doorway appeared the head of a snarling, growling, very angry doberman dog. It curled its lips back and bared a full set of very sharp looking teeth.

Quickly the constable pushed the door shut and jammed a chair up against the handle.

The dog began to growl and bark furiously.

'How did it get out?' asked the constable.

'I don't know, but now we're the ones who are trapped,' the sergeant replied.

'Well, I'll have to go,' said the CID officer and he left the building via the muster room window.

Just then the telephone rang. The sergeant answered it. It was one of the control room staff.

'Sarge, there's a prison siege in Perth. All forces are on stand-by in case extra officers are required to assist.'

'A siege in Perth,' exclaimed the sergeant. 'There's a bloomin' siege along here.'

The sergeant explained the situation and asked for all officers to be warned not to enter the station until the dog had been recaptured.

Just then the police dog handler and some other officers arrived at the back door of the station.

'You'll have to climb through this window,' the sergeant called to them. And so three policemen, one with a dogcatcher's pole, grunted and groaned as they helped each other through the window of the station.

When they were all discussing a plan of attack, they heard the noise of a door banging in the corridor.

It was the door into the public foyer, which had closed behind the dog as it walked through.

The siege was over. The only problem was how to get the dog out of the public foyer.

Taking the sandwiches from his piece box, the sergeant began to throw them to the dog, through the public counter service hatch.

Whilst it was engrossed in its feed, the dog handler was able to place the dogcatcher pole around its neck.

The telephone rang.

'The siege at Perth is over sarge. Your officers won't be required,' said one of the control room staff.

'Aye and it's over here as well,' replied the sergeant as the dog was led from the station.

THE INTERPRETER

A problem arose one morning in the courtroom when the person standing trial turned out to be a German, who could not understand a word of English.

After a discussion between the procurator fiscal and the sheriff, they decided to ask if there was anyone in the courtroom who could speak German.

'I can' said one man sitting in the public gallery. 'I was a prisoner of war during World War II and managed to learn the language of my captors during that time.'

'Very well,' said the sheriff. 'If you would care to come down the procurator fiscal will tell you what to ask the man.'

The man went down and joined the procurator fiscal.

'Ask the man what his name is, please?'

The interpreter cleared his throat and turned to the man standing trial, 'Vot iz yor nem?' he asked in a German accent.

The courtroom was in an uproar. Unfortunately for the interpreter the sheriff was not amused and found him in contempt of court.

HORSE PLAY

Back in the early 1960's an old sergeant took a young probationer out for a foot patrol. As they walked along the streets the sergeant imparted his years of experience and knowledge to the young officer, telling him how to approach different situations should he ever come across them.

Then as they turned around a corner they came across a scene which neither had expected. There in front of them was a horse and cart which was laden with scrap metal and in charge of it all was a very drunk old man.

The sergeant quickly took a hold of the reins of the horse to prevent the horse galloping off down the High Street.

'Here you have a classic case of a man being drunk in charge of a horse and cart,' he informed the probationer. 'Now you escort the oid man back to the station and I'll take the horse and cart back.'

'Do you know how to control it sarge?' asked the probationer.

'Oh I'm sure there's nothing to it,' replied the sergeant, as he climbed up onto the cart.

Giving the horse a few taps with the reins and saying 'Giddi-up Boy' the sergeant attempted to get it moving, but it wouldn't budge. He tried the same method once more and got the same result.

'How do I get this horse of yours to move, old fella?' the sergeant asked the drunk man.

'Just slap it on the backside,' he replied in a slurred voice and then proceeded to do the honours for the sergeant.

The horse took off, taking with it the cart and the sergeant.

Pieces of scrap metal went flying from the cart which was now being pursued by the probationer and some distance behind, a staggering drunk man.

Eventually a shattered sergeant managed to bring the horse and cart to a halt. As the probationer caught up with him he said to the sergeant, 'And here was me thinking you had never done this type of thing before, sarge.'

The sergeant's reply is unrecorded.

BATTERIES NOT INCLUDED

At one station there was concern over an old lady, who for several days had contacted the police regarding the little men who kept appearing in her bedroom at night and keeping her awake with their constant chatting.

Apart from this little problem with her imagination, she was well able to carry out her daily chores. But as the doctor could not provide a solution for the little men one of the seasoned beat men decided to try his own method to provide the old lady with peace of mind.

Taking an empty cardboard box he placed a brick inside it to give it some weight. He taped it shut and then, with a black marker pen, he drew two circles on the front to represent push button controls and a speaker shape above them. The box now looked like an old-fashioned radio.

Taking the box he went along to visit the old lady. He asked her if the little men were still visiting her at night and she told him that they were.

'Well, not for very long,' said the constable as he showed her his new invention. 'This machine will keep them away. All you have to do is press this button at night when you go to your bed and it will send out invisible rays to keep them away.'

The old lady was delighted and put the machine in her bedroom.

Several months passed without any calls being made by the old woman. Then one day she appeared at the station with the machine and asked to see the constable who had given it to her.

The constable came through to see her. 'What's wrong?' he asked her. 'Didn't the machine work?'

'Oh yes,' she replied. 'It was working fine up until last night when the little men came back. I think the battery must be flat. Do you think you could charge it up for me please?'

Paul Christison age 4

A policeman in a bath before going to bed

GETTING A DUSTING DOWN

As a member of the Identification Branch one of my duties is to examine scenes of crime for fingerprints.

One day I received a telephone call from one of my colleagues in the CID asking me to attend at a house, which had been broken into, and dust it for fingerprints.

(The term 'dust it' refers to the method used to find fingerprints, which involves putting aluminium powder onto surfaces which may have fingerprints on it. The powder sticks to the fingerprints making them visible).

I went along to the house concerned and knocked on the door. The door opened and there stood a very large woman, still wearing her nightdress.

'Come in' she said. 'I see they've sent along a young good looking one.'

I opened up my case which contains my equipment.

'I'll start in the living room' I told her.

'Oh I was hoping you were going to say the bedroom' she replied with a devilish smile. 'Would you like a coffee?'

'Yes,' I said, hoping that it would take her out of my way for a few minutes.

I laid my equipment case on the floor and began to dust the window, which had been broken, with aluminium dust. Then I heard her coming through from the kitchen.

'Here's your coffee,' she said.

I turned round to take the cup of coffee but forgot about my equipment case being on the floor and tripped over it.

The tin of aluminium dust flew up into the air and the dust went everywhere. Over me, over her, over the carpet.

I began to apologise profusely but luckily she saw the funny side of it.

'I'll go and get the vacuum cleaner' she said.

I swept some of the dust back into the tin and as I bent over to pick up my case, I felt a vacuum hose pipe running up the inside of my trouser leg.

'I'm just cleaning your trousers' she said. 'What would your wife say if you went home looking like that?'

'What would she say if she saw you do that to me?' I replied.

I finished the job and before leaving I told her to contact my station if she found it necessary to call in a cleaning service, for the mess on her living room carpet.

When I returned to the station I told my inspector what had happened.

'I know already,' he said to me with a grin. 'Your lady friend called to say that she had managed to clean the carpet and offered to do the same for your trousers if you cared to return.'

I declined the offer.

THE POINTSMEN OF PRINCES STREET

It is over twenty years now since traffic lights were installed along Scotland's most famous street, Princes Street.

Before their installation the traffic flow was controlled by a corps of human traffic lights, the Edinburgh city police pointsmen.

Every morning at 8am they could be seen drifting down the side streets in their white coats and taking up their positions at the various junctions on Princes Street, to commence their directional callisthenics. Six hours duty, five days a week.

Given a half an hour break, it was a very long time to stand in all types of weather doing an impression of a human windmill. In winter time conditions could be bleak and with it came wet feet, cold fingers and flu symptoms. In the summer, dust and exhaust fumes could mean headaches, eye problems and a risk of lead poisoning.

So to overcome tedium and prevent the tempers of drivers fraying as traffic built up, the pointsmen introduced humour into the proceedings.

Whilst changing the direction of traffic flow they would perform figure-of-eight turns round the traffic islands or pirouettes between lines of traffic.

One officer, who was a keep-fit fanatic, would execute a sequence of press-ups or burpees during quiet spells. Another would pretend to be pulling the traffic along with an imaginary rope or sweeping it past with an invisible brush.

These antics attracted crowds of people each day during the tourist season and some of the cafes situated above the shops found large queues of people requesting window seats, so that they could enjoy the show whilst having their lunch.

There was one officer who was to become a legend for his zany capers and although he may deny many of the tales told about him, there is definitely 'no smoke without fire'.

He is reported to have directed the traffic on one leg, with the other folded up into the back of his coat, looking like the Long John Silver of pointsmen. On another occasion it is said that due to the volume of traffic, he decided to give the drivers at the end of the queues a better view and stood on top of a traffic island and carried out his signals.

If congestion was slowing down the traffic flow, he would approach a vehicle which had stopped and handed a banana to the driver.

'Would you pass this onto the next pointsman, please. He needs it for his piece break.'

The much bemused driver would carry out the request and hand it over to an equally bemused pointsman at the next junction.

One day during the summer a woman handed a telephone handset to him, saying that it had been wrenched out of a nearby kiosk.

The pointsman put it in his coat pocket and continued with his duties. Some time later, an open top sports car pulled up beside him. Remembering the telephone handset, he made a ringing noise and then pulled the handset out of his pocket.

'Hello. Yes he's here' he said out loud and then turning to the driver of the sports car he handed the handset to him saying, 'It's for you.'

The driver is reported to have put it to his ear and proceed to speak into the mouthpiece.

But my favourite is the day that he was going for his break and passed by a display window of a large department store.

The window had been broken and was being replaced by glaziers. Whilst they had gone to their van to get the new pane of glass, the pointsman jumped inside the display area and took on the pose of a mannequin.

Many passers-by were heard to say, 'How life like it looks,' and one poor woman got the fright of her life when she reached in to find out just how real it was!

But alas in 1970, the District Council erected traffic lights along the street and in doing so brought an end to an era.

Long may they be remembered, the pointsmen of Princes Street.

A HELPING OLD HAND

The divisional commander, a chief superintendent, was nearing his retiral day and there were more than a few grey hairs on his head. (That is on the areas which had hair).

He still loved to get out and about though, just to see how his men were getting on.

One night he decided to tour his division in an unmarked police car and in plain clothes.

As he entered one of the small towns within his division, he heard a call over the radio to the effect that officers required assistance in the town centre, where a large disturbance was taking place.

Always a believer in leading from the front, he sped to the locus of the disturbance. On his arrival there, he jumped out of the vehicle and rendered assistance to his officers who were struggling with several drunk and violent men. Eventually more officers arrived and the situation was returned to normal.

Several men were arrested and taken back to the police station. The chief superintendent followed on.

Once at the station, he brushed himself down and a cup of tea was provided for him. Whilst sitting in the sergeant's office drinking it, he overheard a conversation which made him realise that retirement day wasn't far away.

'Could have been worse,' a young constable said to another.

'At least we got some support from the public this time. Did you see that auld pensioner getting stuck into the fight?'

'SLIDER'

The scene was set, the 1959 Open Golf Championship at the Muirfield Course in Gullane. Gary Player would remember the occasion well, as he became the winner of the world's most prestigious prize in golf that year.

But in all the excitement of the tournament Mr Player and the many golf fans were probably unaware that another event was unfolding. An event which would go down in the annals of police history. Well, at least for one participant it would be remembered to this day.

The weather was glorious and following a long tiresome day on points duty, some of the local officers were told to return to their station.

Before returning, three officers decided to quench their thirst with a bottle of Coke and cool down with an ice-cream.

After making their purchases, the three officers sauntered along the main street, two of them eating their ice-cream 'sliders' (perhaps better known as 'wafers').

As they did so, a chauffeur-driven car passed by. Inside it sat the Chief Constable who, on seeing the three, delivered a stare which was as cold as the ice-cream they were eating.

The three officers knew what lay ahead of them. The next day they were called up to appear in front of the Chief Constable and his senior officers.

They stood to attention in front of the Chief, like lambs to the slaughter.

The Chief did not need to give them an explanation for them being there. They knew and dared not to ask why.

'Well,' said the Chief Constable, staring at the first officer. 'What do you have to say?'

'Sir, I did not have an ice-cream and certainly was not eating one when you passed by,' he replied.

He turned to the second officer. 'And you?'

'Sir, I bought an ice-cream and was going to keep it until I arrived at the station and eat it there. It began to melt, so I decided to lick the melted ice-cream.'

The third constable, a probationer of eight weeks service, cringed as he had thought about using that excuse himself. The Chief must have read his mind.

'Well, son,' the Chief said turning to him. 'You can't use that excuse because yours was half eaten when I saw you. I would imagine that being the youngster in the group it was probably your idea to have an ice-cream.'

The probationer was stunned into silence, which was probably just as well because he wasn't given the chance to speak.

The three officers were given a severe reprimand by the Chief and sent on their way. As they left the room wry smiles appeared on the faces of the senior officers standing behind the Chief.

The two older officers also saw the funny side of it when they got outside. But the poor probationer didn't. He was relieved to still be in a job and when he returned to his station he was called up to appear in front of the chief inspector and sergeant. He received another talking to during which he was given a new nickname.

The nickname stayed with him throughout his thirty years service and even after retiring he was affectionately known as 'SLIDER'.

Grant Menzies age 7

IT'S MURDER OUT THERE

A 999 call came through to one of the officers working within the control room, one morning during the festive season.

'Police, can I help you?' the officer answered.

'Yes, you can,' said a very polite, but also very drunk woman. 'There's been a murder in my front garden.'

The officer called for silence in the room and gave his full attention to the caller.

'Could you tell me what's happened then please?' the officer asked.

'There has been a murder' repeated the woman.

'Who has been murdered and where about?' the officer continued.

'My tortoise has been murdered in my front garden' the woman told him earnestly.

The officer sat back in his chair and breathed a sigh of relief.

Not to offend the woman though he told her, 'I don't think anyone would murder your tortoise madam. Has it not just died through natural causes?'

'No, it has definitely been murdered' the woman insisted.

'And what makes you think that madam?'

'I know it is murder because my tortoise has a noose around it's neck and it wasn't adept at committing suicide,' the woman informed him in a polite but slurred, I-told-you-so voice.

SMOKE GETS IN YOUR EYES

Two police officers received a call to attend at a block of flats where one of the houses was on fire.

They attended immediately and saw smoke coming from a house on the first floor. They were informed by a neighbour that there was someone inside. Without fear for their own safety, they forced open the door of the house and staying low to the floor, they entered the thick grey smoke.

About a minute later they emerged through the smoke, coughing and spluttering, carrying the male occupier of the house. The man was placed into an ambulance and taken to hospital.

Afterwards, whilst the fire service fought the fire, the two officers stood by their panda car coughing and spluttering and rubbing their eyes which were stinging with the effects of smoke.

The sergeant then arrived on the scene and went over to find out how his two officers were.

'Could you help me out sarge?' asked one of the constables with a splutter.

'What is it? Do you want me to get you the oxygen mask?'

'No, no,' said the constable. 'I've run out of cigarettes and I'm desperate for a smoke. Could you give me one?'

BABY TALK

Two officers were on patrol early one morning when they received a call to attend at the local church hall which had been broken into during the night.

When they attended they discovered that every storage cupboard in the hall had been forced open and various items stolen.

Amongst the cupboards entered were the ones used by the Sunday School group and the Boy Scouts.

Items such as a record player, records, books and some sweets were stolen including a large jar of jelly babies.

The officers noted details of the break-in and then began to make an examination of the outside area surrounding the church hall. This is a practice carried out at all break-ins, in order to check for any evidence.

Further up the street from where they were standing, the two officers saw a jelly baby. It was a red one. Then beyond that lay another red one.

The officers started walking towards the jelly babies whereupon they saw more of them, all red ones, lying in a trail along the footway.

They followed the trail until it turned round the corner into another street. There were more, all red ones, and all lying in a trail.

The officers followed the trail until it led them up a garden path and stopped at the front door of a house.

The officers knocked on the door and it was answered by a woman. They learned that the only other person in the house was the woman's son, who was in bed.

She invited them in to speak to her son and in his bedroom they found him sitting beside a record player, records, books and a large storage jar which was half full of jelly babies.

The youth admitted to the officers that he had broken into the church hall and had stolen the property from the cupboards there. As he made his way to his house from the church, he had been eating handfuls of the jelly babies, but because he didn't like the red ones, he had thrown them away.

He hadn't realised that as he walked along throwing the red ones away, he had made a perfect trail for the police to follow.

Who says jelly babies can't talk!

Grant Menzies age 7

'O SOLE MIO'

Due to a spate of housebreakings in the area, police officers on nightshift duty were carrying out a series of road checks in the early hours of the morning.

About 3am two officers set up their road check and shortly after setting it up a car approached them. It was being driven by a male and the vehicle was full of boxes of food and bottles of wine.

The driver of the vehicle rolled his window down.

'Is this your vehicle, sir?' asked one of the officers.

'Yes, officer, it is' said the driver with an Italian accent.

'Tell me sir, why is your car laden with food and drink?'

'Itsa from my restaurant officer. I'ma da owner of the Italiano Restaurante' the driver replied.

'Do you have any identification?' the officer enquired.

The driver searched his pockets and car for identification, but could not find any.

'I'ma sorry officer, but I don't have any.' Then a smile came over the driver's face.

'I know how to prove to you that I'ma da owner of the Italiano Restaurante.' and in full voice he belted out a rendition of *O Sole Mio* (probably better known as 'Just One Cornetto' from the ice-cream advert).

The officers could not believe their ears and fought hard to contain their laughter. After they had verified who the man was, they allowed him to go on his way.

For the next four nights the officers conducted a road check and every night the restaurant owner would approach the check point, stop alongside the officers, roll down the car window and say, 'Itsa only me officers.' and belt out a few lines of *O Sole Mio*.

Then the weekend came and a different pair of officers took over the road check.

About 3am along came the restaurant owner in his car.

'Itsa only me officers. – *O Sole Mio*.'

Unfortunately, the two officers were unaware of this regular event and the Italian restaurant owner was last seen been given a breath-test in the rear of the police car.

A CAUSE FOR ALARM

In part of a building in a back street somewhere in a city, there is a small room which police officers use to have their piece break. In the room there is a sink, small oven and grill, WC and a table and some chairs.

During the piece break the officers would always play cards, brag being the most popular game.

It became so popular back in the early 1960's that off-duty officers would call in during the break to join in the game.

One nightshift two officers returned to the room after having checked the doors and windows of the surrounding shops and offices, to find all the spaces at the table taken up by members of the brag school.

Apart from the officers who were on nightshift there were several off-duty officers, who were on their way home from a party and had called in for a game.

'Sorry, lads, you'll just have to come back for the second break' said one of the men at the table.

This did not please the two officers. They had been out religiously pounding the beat and were cold and hungry.

They left the room and went back out into the cold air of the night.

'I know how we can empty the room' said one of them with a mischievious grin. 'Follow me.'

The two officers headed off down one of the back street lanes.

Looking through some of the rubbish lying about, they found an empty milk bottle and an old alarm clock. Taking this back to the rear of the building where the room was they set to work.

They wound up the spring on the old clock and held the bottle over a rubbish bin. With the help of a brick they smashed the glass bottle and set off the alarm on the old clock. They then ran and hid.

Hearing the sound of breaking glass and a distant alarm ringing, the officers (including the off-duty ones) came running from the room and began to check every window and alarm box in the vicinity. It was a lesson in thoroughness to see them at work. Very commendable too!

When they returned to the police room after checking all the property, they discovered the two jokers tucking into their toasted sandwiches and having a game of brag.

'Hello lads' said one of them. 'You look a bit alarmed. Have we missed something?'

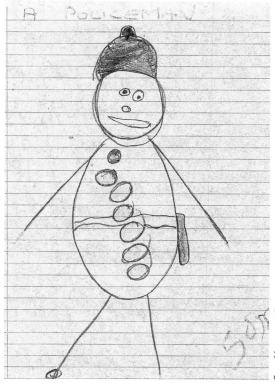

Sam Alcorn age 5

THE WEE HARD MAN WITH A BIG SOFT HEART

No book of police stories would be complete without mentioning the name of the late Willie Merrilees, former Chief Constable of Lothians and Peebles Constabulary.

Willie Merrilees always wanted to be a police officer but due to his lack of inches (he was only 5'6" tall) he was unable to become one.

That was until the day when the Secretary of State waived the minimum height regulation after Willie had made it a regular habit of his, to dive in and rescue people who had fallen into Leith Docks.

As he was considered too small to be a uniformed officer, he was immediately attached to the CID. There he found that his short stature could be used to great advantage, especially when disguising himself in order to apprehend criminals.

On one occasion he disguised himself as a woman in order to catch a bag snatcher.

Another time, he hid himself in a child's pram and lay in wait for a man who had been molesting nannies.

But probably his most daring and dangerous exploit was in September, 1940 when, dressed as a railway porter, he wandered casually into a railway carriage at Edinburgh's Waverley Station and arrested the German spy, Kurt Walther.

Walther, who was armed with a pistol, towered above Merrilees who held on to him with a vice-like grip, preventing him from escaping.

He was appointed as the first Chief Constable of Lothians and Peebles Constabulary in May, 1950, a post he held until he was seventy years of age.

Despite having a reputation as a tough police officer, he was also well known for his charitable work, particularly with the old folk and handicapped children.

He arranged Christmas parties for the young and old and often played the part of Santa at them. He made sure that children whose fathers were imprisoned at Christmas time never went without presents and throughout the year regularly visited Children's Homes taking with him sweets and ice-cream.

He had friends from all walks of life including the late Walt Disney and the famous cowboy Roy Rogers and his wife, Dale Evans. He introduced a young orphan girl to them and Roy and Dale were so taken by her that they decided to adopt her as their own.

Always thinking of others, one day he arrived on the doorstep of a house where officers were about to enter to arrest a man armed with a gun. Willie insisted on going in first, telling his men, 'You've got families to think about.'

Willie Merrilees was a wee hard man with a big soft heart, a man who loved children, and therefore it is only fitting that he receives a mention in a book which has been compiled in aid of a Children's Hospital. I'm sure he would have been proud to be a part of it.

GLOSSARY

ACCUSED	A person alleged to have committed a crime or offence.
ADJOURNED	To put off the hearing of a court case to a future time or date.
AREA	A specific area within a division patrolled by a constable known as an 'area man'.
BACKSHIFT	Period of duty worked by an officer, normally 2pm–10pm.
BARLINNIE	A prison on the west side of Scotland, near Glasgow.
BATON	Part of a police officer's equipment consisting of a length of wood with a leather hand strap which can be used to counter force.
BEAT BOX	Small upright metal unit used by beat men to telephone their stations. (Made famous by Dr Who's Tardis).
BEAT MAN	A constable who patrols a particular section of a city or town.
BOBBY	Nickname for a constable.
BREAK	Period allowed for meals. Also referred to as 'piece break'.
BREATH-TEST	A test conducted on a person suspected of driving a car whilst under the influence of drink sometimes referred to as a breathalyser.
BURPEE	A physical exercise similar to a squat thrust.
CAR MAN	A police officer whose duty involves patrolling a beat or area in a police vehicle.
CELLS	Lockfast rooms approved in law for the detention of arrested persons.
CHIEF CONSTABLE	The most senior police officer within a particular police force.
CHARGED	A term used when an accused person has been cautioned and informed of the particulars in which they will be reported to the courts.
CID	Criminal Investigation Department.
CITATION	A legal form or notice served on a person who is required to attend court as a witness.
CITED	Receiving a court citation.
CLERK/CONTROLLER	A person working within an operations room.

CLERK OF COURT — Responsible for administrative tasks normally within the Sheriff Court.

COMMUNITY BOBBY — Police officer who works in a small town or community.

CONTROL ROOM — Part of a police station where telephone and radio messages are received and dispatched to officers. Also referred to as an ops room/operations room.

COPY COMPLAINT — A notice served on a person who is required to attend court to answer a charge made against them.

COURT CASE — When an accused appears at court to answer a charge against them.

CRIME PATROL — Consists of police officers who patrol in plain clothes.

CUSTODY — When a person has been arrested and detained until their appearance at court.

DAYSHIFT — Period of duty worked by an officer, normally 6am–2pm.

DEATH MESSAGE — Notification of a death relayed by police officers to next of kin.

DEFENCE LAWYER — Legal representative of a person standing trial in a court case.

DIVISIONAL COMMANDER — Senior officer in charge of a division who holds the rank of chief superintendent.

DIVISIONAL HEADQUARTERS — Main station of a division.

DOCK — Position in a court room where an accused person sits during the trial.

DOG HANDLER — Police officer trained to work with a police dog.

DOMESTIC DISPUTE — An argument which takes place within a family home.

DUTY SHEETS — Record of duties performed by officers.

EARLY SHIFT — SEE DAYSHIFT.

EVIDENCE — A means of proving an unknown or disputed fact.

FISCAL (OFFICE) — SEE PROCURATOR FISCAL.

FOUND PROPERTY — Items handed to the police which appear to have been lost by their owner.

GREATCOAT — Heavy woollen coat normally worn by senior police officers.

IDENTIFICATION BRANCH — Part of the Criminal Investigation Branch whose members examine scenes of crime to photograph them and check for fingerprints.

INDICTMENT — A legal document served on a person ordering them to stand trial for a serious crime or offence.

BEAT

INFORMANT	A person who reports a matter to the police.
JUDGE	A person who has been invested with the authority to make a decision on the outcome of a trial and pass sentence.
LEAVE	Allocated holiday period.
LOST PROPERTY	Items left or misplaced by their rightful owner. SEE FOUND PROPERTY.
MESS ROOM	A place where officers rest and take their refreshment break.
M'LORD	A term used to address a judge or sheriff.
MOT TEST	A test required on motor vehicles over three years of age for road worthiness.
MOTOR CYCLE OFFICER	Police officers attached to the Traffic Department who patrol on motor cycles.
NIGHTSHIFT	Period of duty worked by an officer, normally 10pm–6am.
PANDA	A term given to police patrol vehicles initially derived from the black and white markings similar to those of a panda.
PIECE	Food eg sandwiches taken at meal breaks.
PIECE BREAK	Time allocated for meals.
PLAIN CLOTHES	An officer working in civilian clothing instead of a uniform is said to be in 'plain clothes'.
POACHERS	A person involved in the unlawful capture and destruction of game.
PROBATIONER CONSTABLE	A police constable within the two year initial training period.
PROCURATOR FISCAL	A lawyer within Scotland whose responsibilities include public prosecutor within the District and Sherriff Courts. Part of the Civil Service.
SEARCH TEAM	A group of trained police officers used in different types of searches.
SENT DOWN	Slang for prison sentence.
SENTENCE	A definite judgement pronounced by a trial judge in a civil or criminal court.
SERGEANT	A rank designated by chevrons or stripes on the sleeves of a police officer.
SHERIFF	Generally used to describe a person who acts as a judge in the Sheriff Court.

SHERIFF CLERK	SEE CLERK OF COURT.
SHERIFF COURT	Courts situated within Scotland with a sheriff in charge of the trial.
SHIFT	Hours of duty performed by a police officer. Also a group of police officers who work together on a regular basis. Can also be referred to as a 'team'.
SSPCA	Scottish Society for the Prevention of Cruelty to Animals.
SUMMATION SHEET	All incidents considered of importance that occur during a specific 24 hour period.
TEAM	SEE SHIFT.
TRAFFIC PATROL CAR	High power police motor vehicles.
TRAFFIC PATROL OFFICER	A police officer trained to a very high standard in driving motor vehicles.
TRIAL	The examination of circumstances, civil or criminal, brought before a trial judge who has jurisdiction over it.
TUTOR	A police officer entrusted in giving guidance to a probationer during their initial months of training.
UNDERWATER RESCUE TEAM	Police officers trained to carry out specific underwater diving duties.
VETTING OFFICER	Normally a civilian employee responsible for visiting applicants who wish to join the police force at their homes and collating background information on them.
WITNESS BOX	Part of a court room a witness stands or sits to give evidence.